THE RE-ENCHANTMENT OF THE WORLD

The
Re-enchantment
of the World

Art versus Religion

The Stanton Lectures in the Philosophy of Religion delivered at the
University of Cambridge

GORDON GRAHAM

OXFORD
UNIVERSITY PRESS

OXFORD
UNIVERSITY PRESS

Great Clarendon Street, Oxford OX2 6DP

Oxford University Press is a department of the University of Oxford.
It furthers the University's objective of excellence in research, scholarship,
and education by publishing worldwide in

Oxford New York

Auckland Cape Town Dar es Salaam Hong Kong Karachi
Kuala Lumpur Madrid Melbourne Mexico City Nairobi
New Delhi Shanghai Taipei Toronto

With offices in

Argentina Austria Brazil Chile Czech Republic France Greece
Guatemala Hungary Italy Japan Poland Portugal Singapore
South Korea Switzerland Thailand Turkey Ukraine Vietnam

Oxford is a registered trade mark of Oxford University Press
in the UK and in certain other countries

Published in the United States
by Oxford University Press Inc., New York

British Library Cataloguing in Publication Data

Data available

Library of Congress Cataloging in Publication Data

Data available

Typeset by Laserwords Private Limited, Chennai, India
Printed in Great Britain
on acid-free paper by
Biddles Ltd., King's Lynn, Norfolk

ISBN 978-0-19-926596-1

1 3 5 7 9 10 8 6 4 2

For my son Magnus who was born just as this book was completed

Contents

Preface and Acknowledgements

The subject of this book—the relation that exists between art and religion and its contemporary cultural relevance—has generated a very large literature to which artists, theologians, cultural historians, and sociologists have contributed. Somewhat surprisingly, however, it is a literature to which philosophers have added relatively little. Indeed, while 'art and ethics' and 'art and politics' are now standard topics in philosophical aesthetics, most of the major handbooks and companions to aesthetics published since the 1980s have no entry or essay entitled 'art and religion', or even any significant entries on religion in their indices.

It is not obvious why this should be the case, but, whatever its explanation, it gives grounds for hope that this book, though on a well-worn subject, may yet have something new to say just because it takes a philosophical approach. The guarantee that its approach is properly regarded as philosophical lies in the fact that the most influential figures behind it are Hegel, Schopenhauer, and Nietzsche. It is their writings that provide the context in which I have found it most profitable to think. All of them are usually regarded as 'Continental' philosophers, whereas by education and orientation I would be classified as an 'analytic' philosopher. But a further hope is that the argument I develop shows this distinction to be uninformative and even unhelpful. A philosophical treatment of art and religion that aims to offer something substantial and interesting to the debates that surround these concepts is better off ignoring it.

This book is the third in an investigation I have been engaged in for a long time. Its purpose is a philosophical assessment of the extent to which religious ideas continue to underlie some of the central concepts of contemporary culture, and what this means for secular versions of those concepts. In *The Shape of the Past* (Oxford University Press, 1997) I explored ways of appropriating history so that it becomes our past. In *Evil and Christian Ethics* (Cambridge University Press, 2001) my concern was with the theological underpinnings of morality. The aim of this volume is to consider the arts from the same point of view.

The larger part of the text consists in a revised version of the Stanton Lectures in Philosophy and Religion that I gave at the University of Cambridge in 2005 under the title 'Art in an Irreligious World'. I was honoured by my election to this long-established lectureship, and most grateful to members of the Faculty of Divinity, especially Professor Denys Turner and Dr Douglas Hedley, for their welcome and hospitality, as also to the Revd Ian Thompson, Dean of King's College. I gladly acknowledge a Research Leave Grant from the Arts and Humanities Research Council that enabled me to devote my time exclusively to preparing the lectures.

Between the Stanton Lectures and the preparation of the book, I left the University of Aberdeen for Princeton Theological Seminary. This enabled me to offer a doctoral seminar on Philosophy, Art, and Culture at the same time as I was working on the typescript, and I want to record the great benefit I derived from discussing these subjects with the graduate students in that seminar. A full draft was completed during the summer of 2006 in New College Edinburgh, where Professor David Fergusson kindly arranged for me to have an office and Research Visitor status, and was subsequently revised in the light of helpful comments from the anonymous readers for Oxford University Press.

A small part of the text was previously published in the third edition of *Philosophy of the Arts* (Routledge, 2005) and in the *Journal of Aesthetics and Art Criticism* in an article entitled 'Can there be Public Architecture?'

Gordon Graham

Princeton, 2007

1

Spheres of Meaning

IDEALISM

An ancient approach to philosophy begins with the question of what it is that marks human beings off from other kinds of being. An equally ancient answer, Plato's in fact, draws a sharp contrast between physical and mental being, or body and soul, and locates the distinctiveness of human beings in the latter. There thus enters into philosophy at a very early stage a kind of dualism, and it is not entirely fanciful to regard the subsequent history of the subject as a repeated attempt to deal with this dualism—by affirming it, denying it, or overcoming it in some way.

The most metaphysically weighty form of affirming dualism construes it as an ontological distinction that posits two different kinds of 'stuff', a mental and a physical 'substance' of some sort. The most trenchant metaphysical alternative denies the reality of the distinction by explaining one side as a manifestation of the other. Occasionally, as in Plato perhaps and Bishop Berkeley, philosophers have attempted to reduce the physical to the mental, but, much more commonly, the mental is reduced to the physical and thought of as a phenomenal manifestation of it. It is plausible to suggest, in my view, that no one has ever been much persuaded by the first of these reductions. In sharp contrast, the second is widely taken to be obviously correct. That is why in the modern period the debate about mind and body has generally been couched in terms of just two possibilities—dualism and physicalism. The principal difficulty confronting the first is well known. If mind and body (or thought

and extension) are ontologically distinct, how is it possible for there
to be any relation between them? Yet it is precisely in trying to
arrive at an adequate understanding of this relation that dualism
was posited in the first place. The principal difficulty confronting
the second is that any reduction of the mental to the physical risks
the elimination of the mental altogether, so that the appeal to the
physical as the ultimate *explanans* results not so much in explaining
the mental as in explaining it *away*.

The philosophy known as Idealism, whose origins lie in Kant, but
which found its most influential form in Hegel, represents the third
possibility—neither affirming nor denying, but *overcoming* the dualism of mind and body. No doubt there are many variations between
all those authors and positions that are labelled 'Idealist', but the
version I have chiefly in mind is that which was prominent in Britain
and North America in the late nineteenth century (conveniently
summarized in Edward Caird's British Academy Lecture 'Idealism
and the Theory of Knowledge'). Its collapse was rather sudden. In
the first decades of the twentieth century, a powerful combination
of logical positivism and native British empiricism brought about
the virtual demise of Idealism within Anglo-American philosophy.
Both R. G. Collingwood and Michael Oakeshott are interesting
thinkers and significant continuers of the spirit of Idealist philosophy, but for the larger part of the twentieth century neither had much
impact on English language philosophy. Compared to the position
in 1900, and despite great interest in Kant, Idealism acknowledged
as such made scarcely any appearance in the philosophical landscape
of 2000. The principal twentieth-century alternative to analytical
debates dominated by dualism and reductionism was 'Continental'
philosophy, a mix of Marxism, Existentialism, Structuralism, Fem-
inism, and Postmodernism. It is thanks to this alternative strand
of thought that major thinkers such as Hegel and Nietzsche came
to be given the attention they deserve. Unhappily, this led to
them being identified with an anti-analytical philosophical orientation, so that, although they unquestionably stand in the tradition
of Plato, Aristotle, Descartes, Kant, and so on, the illumination

they offer on some of the recurrent problems of analytical philosophy has been overlooked. This book is based on the thought that, by revisiting Idealism, something of this illumination can be recovered.

The book is not an essay in the philosophy of mind, however, and so I shall not be concerned to re-visit Idealism with a view to throwing new light on the mind/body problem. From an Idealist point of view, mind/body is just one duality that needs to be overcome. There are many others that have set philosophy's agenda, of which freedom and causality, the subjective and the objective, consciousness and content, fact and value, are among the most important. For my purposes all these can be subsumed under a general distinction offered to us by Hegel, the distinction between Nature and Spirit (words I shall capitalize when using them in this quasi-technical sense). Expressed in this way, we might describe the general course of philosophy as a debate between those who want to spiritualize Nature (pantheists, including Spinoza perhaps), those who want to naturalize Spirit (naturalists, like Hume and Mill say), and those who hold that there is a radical gulf between the two (Cartesians). The key thought in Idealism (as I understand it) is that all these positions mistakenly treat the distinctions they employ as absolute. That is to say, they hold that the last word (so to speak) in metaphysics must lie with one, or the other, or both equally. Either to be *is* to be perceived (Berkeley, Kant on some interpretations), or mind is fully explained in terms of matter in motion (Hobbes and modern materialists), or mind and matter are ontologically distinct (Plato/Descartes). None of these is ultimately satisfactory, the Idealist contends, because either they require us to deny the reality of some aspect of our experience outright, or they elevate the distinctions we commonly draw to a level that makes our experience incoherent. Human beings intuitively draw distinctions between mind and body, free will and causality, subject and object, and so on, while at the same time employing these distinctions in a way that presupposes a relation between them. The philosophical task is to make *both* the distinction *and* the relation intelligible.

This task, however, is not a purely intellectual one. The oppositions that comprise Spirit and Nature confront us in active life. Freedom implies responsibility, causality denies it. Thus, understanding the relation between them properly is of crucial importance to morality and the law. At a very basic level, the confrontation between Nature and Spirit may just be between the individual will and the intractable material world it encounters. I decide to go from A to B and find my path blocked by a river. My successfully getting to the other side requires that I do more than merely imagine I am there. But neither must I accept the reality of the river as an insurmountable obstacle. By means of practical deliberation and creative imagination, I devise a way of getting to the other side. The river continues to exist, of course, but the *river as obstacle,* to my will and desire, has been overcome.

This example will serve to illustrate some further important aspects of the Idealist way of thinking. One obvious way of overcoming the river as obstacle is to build a bridge. But the technology of bridge building is a cultural accumulation; the practical deliberation and creative imagination of the individual are never sufficient to come up with such a solution *de novo*. This cultural accumulation is twofold, conceptual as well as material. It consists both in the very idea of bridging a river, and in the actual technology that allows us to build bridges successfully. The conceptual and the material are inseparable, and together they are the product of a cultural history. History in this sense is not merely the passage of time, but the accumulated thought and experience of a set of people whose identity arises precisely from a past commonly acknowledged as *theirs* (more often implicitly than explicitly). This historical dimension is an aspect of Idealism that is to be returned to shortly.

As it stands, this particular example simply takes it as a fact that I want to cross the river. My desire to do so might be nothing more than an impulse that I find myself having, something like the desire that impels an animal to roam for food. A distinguishing mark of human consciousness, however, lies in its being subject to its own critical reflection: is crossing the river a good idea, and if so, why?

Once begun, this process of reflection moves imperceptibly to ever larger interests and concerns—from action to purpose to plan to strategy to goal—and at the furthest point results in the question 'What am I to make of my life?', a question inseparable from a closely related one: '*How* am I to make something of my life?' Both these questions point us to an important Idealist concept—self-realization.

The aim of self-realization has often been misunderstood. Either it is thought to bring with it too much in the way of metaphysical baggage, or it is discounted as little more than a grandiose term for moral self-indulgence. But it is worth persisting with because it captures something of considerable philosophical importance. What am I going to *make* of my life? What am I going to *be*? These are both ontological questions in the sense that they refer to something coming or being brought into existence. But the 'being' they refer to—the person I am or become—does not fall on either side of the body/mind distinction. Nor is it some unhappy division between the two. A 'life' in this sense is not merely a biological event, as the 'life' of a tree might be said to be. But neither is it a 'mental' event such as a separable stream of thought or consciousness, which is how Cartesian ways of thinking tend to represent it. What I *am* includes but overcomes (or in Hegelian language 'sublates') the division between body and mind, thought and extension. Human beings are *both* Spirit and Nature. Self-realization may be described as the achievement of a mode of being within which they can properly cohere. In the course of a human life a self is realized, made a thing. This self, however, is not properly conceived (as Hobbesian egoists may be said to conceive it) in terms of a bundle of felt desires that await satisfaction. To think in this way is to slide into according absolute status to one side of another duality (reason and feeling, objective/subjective) so that, in a famous phrase of Hume's, reason is conceived as the slave of the passions. But I can *decide* what I want to be. Importantly, though, while I can decide what I want to be, I cannot decide the constitution of the thing that I want to be. My subjective desire is formed in the light of objective purposes.

For example, suppose I want to be a doctor. This is a subjective desire in the sense that I experience it. But the *object* of the desire 'being a doctor' exists independently of my desire. What it is to be a doctor is not a matter of my making. Successfully becoming a doctor thus has both a subjective and an objective side. On the subjective side, my desire is fulfilled rather than frustrated; on the objective side I truly am a doctor, and do not merely fancy myself to be so. There is thus a consonance between what I want to do and what being a doctor requires me to do, a consonance that should make thought and feeling and action cohere into a unity. This unifying coherence is what the idea of self-realization is meant to capture. At the same time, being a doctor cannot be conceived as a complete form of self-realization, because, though being a doctor is more than just a job, it describes a professional occupation rather than a full human life. Any actual doctor has more than a professional life. Family, friends, hobbies, and so on will all play an important part in his or her life story. Standardly, however, these other aspects of life are not merely distinguishable, but largely separate. The hopes, ambitions, and accomplishments relevant to each have relatively little to do with the others.

This separation becomes a matter of consequence for us when we are compelled to ask just what aspect of our lives it is that ultimately makes them worth living. Pressed to an answer, we are likely to find that the personal and the professional offer independent, and sometimes competing, answers. According to Alasdair MacIntyre, this is not an inescapable feature of the human condition, but a marked feature of modernity.

Any contemporary attempt to envisage each human life as a whole, as a unity . . . encounters two different kinds of obstacle, one social and one philosophical. The social obstacles derive from the way in which modernity partitions each human life into a variety of segments, each with its own norms and modes of behaviour. So work is divided from leisure, private life from public, the corporate from the personal. So both childhood and old age have been wrenched away from the rest of human life and made over into distinct realms. . . . The philosophical obstacles derive from two distinct tendencies . . . [first] the tendency to think atomistically about human action and analyse complex actions and transactions in terms of social components . . . [and second] . . . when a sharp separation is made either between the individual and the roles that he or she plays . . . or between the different roles—and quasi-role enactments of an individual life so that life comes to appear as nothing but a series of unconnected episodes. (MacIntyre 1981: 190)

The theme is one to be returned to, but for present purposes it is relevant to note that religion stands in contrast to this modern tendency because of its unifying character. To be a Christian, a Muslim, or a Jew is an identity that (in theory at any rate) touches and informs all aspects of a life. This is why it is useful to distinguish between 'occupation' and 'vocation'. As I intend the term, a vocation offers us the possibility of a unified life, that is to say, a life in which all the different aspects cohere. The connection with religion lies in the fact that the word 'vocation' has a theological root, and refers to being called by God. But, in contemporary usage, and for some considerable time, it has been possible to speak of vocations in wider contexts, and with different objects in view. It is in this non-theological sense that Max Weber writes of 'Science as a Vocation' and 'Politics as a Vocation'. 'Science' and 'Politics' are two very general abstract concepts that naturally fall alongside a number of others—'art', 'religion', and 'morality' being further obvious instances. All these can be thought of as cultural spheres, and it is not implausible to think of realizing a meaningful life as finding a vocation within one of them—as artist, scientist, politician. It is also plausible to think that one such sphere encompasses the others within it; religion has often been thought of in this way—a Jewish politician, a Christian artist, and so on. Similarly, the concept of human beings as moral agents is often thought to be more fundamental or encompassing than their roles as artists or scientists. Conceived in this way, the concept of vocation is contentious, however. Discussing this issue in the context of art, Jacques Barzun writes: 'It is part of the loss of faith generally . . . [that the] very word vocation can nowadays only be spoken with irony: we are not called in the least' (Barzun 1974: 92).

One way of summarizing the issue this book addresses would be as follows: can human beings find a properly encompassing vocation in art or the aesthetic? For the moment, then, the term 'vocation' will have to be used in inverted commas, and the expression 'spheres of meaning' will have to be used with similar caution. But, in the light of this qualification, let us say that among such spheres of meaning we may include science, art, religion, politics, morality, and perhaps others (sport?), and that to describe them in this way is to say that any of them may offer human beings the possibility of a unifying 'vocation', a way of realizing a meaningful life.

It is characteristic of a good deal of Idealist philosophy, starting with Hegel, that it casts its thought in terms of these general concepts, a style of reflection that has influenced important thinkers who cannot themselves be classified as Idealists, still less Hegelians. Both Schopenhauer and Kierkegaard are among Hegel's fiercest critics (the former hating him with a passion) and yet both use the concepts of the aesthetic, the ethical, and the religious to depict alternative aspects/kinds of life. Similarly, Nietzsche's central theses, especially in *Human, All Too Human*, would be impossible to state except in terms of such general concepts as 'morality', 'religion', and 'art'. At the same time, philosophy conducted after this fashion (as I too propose to conduct it) must find a way round certain important difficulties.

The first of these is method. According to Plato's account of it, the Socratic dialectic seeks to understand such general concepts by means of definition, and the pursuit of adequate definition is still a marked feature of some branches of philosophy—aesthetics, for example. Leaving aside the fact that no proposed definition ever seems to meet with widespread agreement, there is this further problem. If we arrive at a definition of Art or Religion that can accommodate all or most of the phenomena that people are inclined to classify under these labels, the definition will be too abstract to do any useful work as far as critical application goes. If, alive to this danger, we approach the task from the other direction, start with the phenomena that are classified in these ways and try to generalize from them, we will find that the variety is too great to uncover anything common to all. The first may be said to be the error into which Platonism falls, the second the outcome of an empirical approach.

A second problem is that of normativity. What is the purpose of a philosophical definition? At least part of the purpose is the desire to tell the true from the false, the real from the unreal. We want to know whether all that passes for religion, or science, or art is properly so called. Is Wicca a religion? Is psychoanalysis a science? Can ready-mades be works of art? And so on. These are often questions of considerable importance beyond philosophy. Should research in psychoanalysis be financially supported by foundations devoted to the advancement of science? Should Wicca be accorded the same legal status as other religions? Should the purchase of ready-mades qualify for grants from a foundation devoted to the arts? But how could a philosophical definition abstractly arrived at have any authority in this respect? Suppose that, on one proposed definition of 'science', physics should turn out not to be a science. Or, on a proposed definition of religion, Buddhism should turn out not to be a religion. Would there not then be greater reason to reject the definition than to apply it?

The answer to this question seems obvious, and this suggests that all such definitions must answer to the facts, so that the empirical alternative beckons once more. But this will not do for a related reason. The normative question—is this science?—cannot be answered on the strength of the 'facts' because the facts are contentious. The proponents of psychoanalysis will undoubtedly claim the status of science for it, just as Karl Popper famously denied it, and adherents of Wicca will declare it to be truly a religion in order to put themselves on a par with Christians, Jews, and Muslims. When Duchamps offered a urinal to an exhibition in New York, the question could not be avoided—is this art or not? But the only way to answer it, it seems, is to answer the abstract question—what *is* art?

CONCEPTUAL HISTORY

One of the merits of Idealism, in my estimation, lies in its ability to give us a way round this impasse. It does so by drawing attention to an important fact. Plato was mistaken in thinking of concepts as the names of Forms or Ideas that are both unchanging and of universal validity. This is because almost all the concepts we employ have a history. They are not of our own invention, but have come down to us from the past. This is not just a remark about language. The Italian word *scienza* and the German word *Wissenschaft* both have a history. Lexicographers can put fairly precise dates on their first appearances. But these different words capture the same concept— 'science'—and this *concept* also has a history. That is to say, it is the origins not only of the word, but of the idea it seeks to capture and express, that we can identify. The history of the concept 'science', however, is not just a matter of origins. We can also trace its evolutionary development over a long period. This is perhaps the most important and enduring lesson to be learned from Hegel's philosophy, and a salutary counter to Platonism; the history of ideas is that of an unfolding development (*Entwicklung*). That is to say, the concepts we employ embody the state of our understanding and inform our activity in its light. As time passes, human understanding develops, becoming more sophisticated and changing our activity accordingly. One aspect of this development is the emergence of new concepts; another is the disappearance of old ones. For example, there was a time when the concept of 'germ', now so crucial to medical science and the practice of healing, was unknown, and, conversely, the concepts of 'witch' and 'phlogiston', once widely used, have (for rather different reasons) become redundant. All the phenomena to which these concepts related are better understood now than they were, and that is why such changes have taken place. Human understanding, then, has a history in which concepts come and go. They can also become more refined and precise; the disappearance of the concept of 'witch' is part of the same history in which the related concept of 'wickedness' has become more refined.

Looking back to the Greeks, it is evident that this kind of conceptual evolution has been central to intellectual activity and to the development of disciplined enquiry. In the fragmentary writings of the pre-Socratics we find the beginnings of what we now distinguish as 'science' and 'philosophy', but we find them inextricably intermingled with religious and theological interests and conceptions. It is pointless to ask whether the pre-Socratics were philosophers, scientists, or theologians. They were all and none of these things, since the attempt to apply these distinctions as we now make them is anachronistic. The concepts of philosophy, theology, and science have evolved (or in more Hegelian language unfolded) from this shared beginning, and discrimination between them is possible now where previously it was not.

Exactly the same is true in the case of Art and Religion, the concepts with which this book is concerned. One of the sins 'endemic to philosophically minded art theory' Karol Berger remarks, is that it 'speaks ahistorically as if art (or rather Art) were a permanent unchanging feature of human nature, rather than a culturally evolving practice or family of practices' (Berger 2000: 109). We think of Sophocles as a great dramatist or playwright and consequently classify *Oedipus Rex* alongside *Hamlet* and *Lear*. Yet we might as readily describe him as a great liturgist. To do so would sound very odd, but 'liturgist' is actually no odder than the anachronistic 'playwright'. As is well known, Greek tragedies were written for and performed at religious festivals in which music played an important part. They thus share features *both* with major Christian observances like Midnight Mass at Christmas, *and* with a night at the opera. Since we now regard these as importantly different, it is tempting to identify Greek tragedies with one or the other (usually opera-type performance), but the truth is that they cannot be exclusively identified with either.

This point about conceptual evolution is especially important for the issue of art's relation to religion. Music, sculpture, poetry, and architecture were all to be found in the ancient world, as they are in ours. We commonly gather these individual arts (along with some others) within the general concept 'Art'. But, as has often been observed, the Greeks, indeed the ancients, had no word for 'Art'. The Greek word *techne* is not accurately translated in this way or even the Latin word *ars* despite its etymological association. It is less often observed that a similar point can be made about religion. Histories and guidebooks tell us about 'the religion of the ancient Greeks', and it is true that they had temples, gods, and stories of their doings on Olympus. Greek 'religion' was not like Judaism, however. Still less did it have the scope or coherence of Christianity or Islam, and the distinctions that are now important, between religion, magic, myth, superstition, and political ceremony, cannot be drawn meaningfully within it. Of course, we have to describe their culture in some way if we are to say anything about it, and speaking of Greek art and Greek religion need not be dramatically misleading. Nevertheless, it should constantly be remembered that the concepts of art and religion have evolved just as much as the concepts of science and medicine have. This is why the attempt to define them as though they were Platonic Forms or natural kinds has always proved a failure.

At the same time, we should not conclude from this (as some have done) that philosophy has to give way to the history of ideas. Historical understanding seeks to explain phenomena in terms of origins—by 'going back to the beginning'. By contrast, Hegel's celebrated dictum that 'the owl of Minerva takes its flight at dusk' positions understanding at the end of a process, not at the start. That is why 'development' is a more accurate translation of Hegel's *Entwicklung* than 'evolution'. Hegel thinks philosophical understanding requires hindsight, a view of the past from the vantage point of the present. To take the example of the pre-Socratics again: we are able to understand the mixture of science, philosophy, and religion that pervades their thought in a way that they could not have, precisely because we have the benefit of operating with these as distinct concepts. This enables us to see (among other things) not

just why they thought the things that they did, but where they went
wrong in thinking them.

What is crucial to Idealism, as I understand it, is its pursuit of a
genuinely philosophical understanding that, because it looks from
present to past rather than from past to present, is informed by
history, but not itself merely historical. This is an interpretation
the nineteenth-century Scottish Idealist David Ritchie confirms in
a paper originally read to the Aristotelian Society in 1891, whose
point was to explore the similarities and differences between Darwin
and Hegel: 'The Idealist . . . insists that, after we have as complete a
history as can be given of how things have come to be what they
are, we are justified in looking back from our vantage point and
seeing in the past evolution the gradual "unrolling" of the meaning
that we only fully understand at the end of the process' (Ritchie
1893/1998: 75–6).

An instructive example that serves to illuminate the contrast is
Larry Shiner's *The Invention of Art*, an account of the gradual
emergence of the concept of 'art' as we know it today. Though
himself a philosopher, he subtitles his book 'a cultural history',
thereby seeming to identify it as a study of the past. At the same
time, the book has a normative tone. There is an unspoken suggestion
in the way he writes, and even in the title, that 'art' is a manufactured
concept, not grounded in reality somehow, a kind of chimera that
haunts the intellectual world in a way that 'philosophy' or 'science'
does not. 'The Greeks had no word for it' is in fact the heading
he gives to the first section of his opening chapter. But the Greeks
had no word for lots of things whose reality is not in doubt, so
that there is no immediate implication to be drawn about art in
particular. What is true, though, is that 'art' is an emergent concept.
Its emergence or 'invention' does not make it any less substantial.
This shows that the concept is not fixed, but contains the seeds
of its development within it. Calling something 'Art' marks an
aspiration as well as a reality. While the investigation of its origins
and development can be undertaken out of interest in the history
of ideas, there is thus this further matter of aspiration. Assessing its

realism is a task for normative philosophical enquiry, and part of the importance of examining the concept's historical development lies in the value it has for this enquiry. The question is whether a concept of Art has emerged from this evolutionary history that is coherent, or whether the elements within it conflict in some way. Shiner's is an important and insightful book to which we will return, and in fact the normative question is one he is concerned to address. But his description of it as 'a cultural history' is misleading with respect both to the book itself, and to the contemporary cultural significance of the kind of investigation it is.

The Hegelian account of philosophical development might seem reasonably uncontentious in the case of art (though there is a good deal more to be said about it). But if the point about evolutionary development applies in general, something similar has to be said about religion—that 'religion' too is an emergent concept. This is an unfamiliar thought nowadays, though nineteenth-century Idealists (and others) developed it at length, as, for example, in Edward Caird's Gifford Lectures *The Evolution of Religion*. The idea at work in his lectures is that the concept of 'religion' captures first and foremost, not a specific historical phenomenon or set of phenomena, but an aspiration of the human mind and spirit. Religious activity is a kind of 'striving towards the complete realization of itself' (Caird 1907: i. 35). Crucially this striving includes within it an attempt to understand more adequately what it is a striving for, or, as Caird puts it, the history of religion is one in which it is 'progressively defining itself' (ibid. i. 61). This is why later forms of religion are more articulate than earlier ones; they are more self-conscious. An important implication of this is that studying the evolution of religion is important, not just because of the intrinsic interest of the process, but because of its ability to help us address our own religious questions. In his preface, Caird declares that a major part of the point of his lectures is to enable 'that large and increasing class who have become . . . alienated from the ordinary dogmatic system of belief . . . to distinguish what is tenable from what is untenable in the opposite claims made upon them' (ibid. i, pp. viii–ix) by Christians and sceptics.

So too 'the invention of art' arises from a kind of striving—the attempt to develop out of the mechanical arts and the skills that their mastery has won, an autonomous realm of activity that will transform those same skills in ways that realize their potential more fully. 'A practice is autonomous', Berger writes, 'because it has aims of its own and does not derive them from another practice' (Berger 2000: 115). The Greeks, it is true, had no word for 'art' in this sense, because the *techne* with which they were familiar derived its meaning from the practice of making and fashioning in general. Nevertheless, the concepts of *ars* and *techne* contain elements that are still to be found in 'art' as we now think of it (the 'art' of the ready-made aside, for the moment). The philosophical question is whether they have acquired aims of their own sufficiently distinct and coherent to allow us to say that Art's 'striving towards the complete realization of itself' has been successful.

SPHERES OF MEANING

The position we have reached is this. Human beings, unlike other animals, seek more than health, satisfaction, and longevity. They also seek meaningful lives. The accomplishment of a meaningful life can be conceived as a process of self-realization; the different aspects of a human life—reason, emotion, desire, accomplishment, work, leisure, personal relationships, and so on—are successfully forged into a coherent whole. Let us call any mode of existence in which such a self can be realized a 'vocation'. Vocations depend on spheres of meaning—Art, Politics, Religion, Science, Morality—each of which is a developed cultural entity, part practice and artefacts, part philosophical idea, the idea being the aspiration embodied in the practices and their products. These cultural entities have to be historically and socially specific. Having identified one of the besetting sins of the philosophically minded art theorist, Berger identifies another that 'speaks of Art, rather than concrete specific arts, even though more often than not one does have one specific art, and not Art in general at the back of one's mind. (Thus when Dewey speaks of art he usually means painting, just as Heidegger usually means poetry)' (Berger 2000: 109). A parallel point can be made about 'religion'. It can be useful to talk of 'Religion' quite generally (as Schleiermacher does in his early *Speeches*), but all its historical manifestations are particular religions—Christianity, Islam, Hinduism, and so on.

One merit of Hegel's philosophy of art (as opposed to Kant's, say), is that he cannot be said to fall into the sin that Berger identifies. In his *Lectures on Aesthetics* he devotes almost the whole of the second half to a treatment of the specific forms of art—architecture, sculpture, painting, music, poetry, and drama. His treatment of them, however, is set within a much larger context in which he attempts to relate the general spheres of art, religion, and philosophy. By his account, all these are spheres within which Spirit seeks to realize itself. The 'motor' that drives this quest is the need to overcome its opposition to Nature, and progress takes the form of the celebrated Hegelian dialectic—thesis–antithesis–synthesis. The various art forms can be hierarchically ordered in accordance with the extent to which they more adequately allow the realization of Spirit. Thus, painting is more adequate to Spirit than sculpture because (roughly) its figures are images not objects.

But it is not just the various arts that can be ordered hierarchically. So too can the spheres of meaning. What Art strives to do finds a more adequate mode of realization in Religion, and the ambition within Religion is realized most satisfactorily in Philosophy. All this can sound extravagant, though Hegel's thinking on these matters is not as fanciful (or obscure) as is often alleged. What matters more for present purposes, however, is the lead he gave in trying to relate these 'spheres of meaning' in an intelligible and illuminating way. The nineteenth century saw the emergence of three important rival views, all of which are conceived along broadly similar lines. Marx, Hegel's most famous critic, claimed to 'turn him on his head', but his concern was still with the ways in which Spirit can be realized. For Marx, though, it is the human spirit not Absolute Spirit that seeks realization. Religion is an 'opiate' that loses its value once the painful condition of human alienation is overcome, and Art is of purely instrumental value in this quest for human freedom that will ultimately be satisfied only in communist society. Kierkegaard, another of Hegel's critics, contrasts the aesthetic and the religious way of life and (at least in some moods) places the second above the first. Both contend with a third possibility—ethical life—while the philosophical (or scientific) sphere of meaning is rejected altogether because for Kierkegaard it does not constitute a sphere of meaning by which we could live. This is the force of his celebrated slogan 'Truth as Subjectivity'. Nietzsche, another major post-Hegelian thinker, makes very few explicit references to Hegel. Yet he also thinks in the same general way. 'Morality' for Nietzsche is a defective sphere of meaning, a mode of slave mentality, while Art and Religion encapsulate rival attitudes to life.

Hegel and Kierkegaard, for rather different reasons, rank Religion above Art. Nietzsche sees Art as increasingly occupying the place of Religion. His view, in contrast to theirs, appears to reflect more accurately an observable tendency, and one that the next chapter will address. But, whichever view we take in the end, there is a good case to be made for thinking that Art and Religion are closely allied in some way or other. In their most developed forms both make important use of three concepts, namely 'creation', 'inspiration', and 'contemplation'. God is a creator, and his creative acts both invite our contemplation and inspire us. Something very similar is commonly said of art and artists—that artworks are also the outcome of creativity and objects worthy of studied contemplation. They are also commonly said to be both inspired and inspiring.

This conceptual overlap can hardly be a matter of pure contingency. And, indeed, it is not. As Christopher Sartwell remarks, 'the history of Western art is *incomprehensible* without an account of Western religion' (Levinson 2003: 762; emphasis added). An important part of this history over the last 200 years or so, is an ambition on the part of art to retain its importance while winning its autonomy from religion. If this is true, it can hardly come as a surprise that, at some level or other, the two are in competition. If Hegel is right, Art is bound to lose this competition. If Nietzsche is right, Art can present itself in this way only because Religion has already lost it. It is the principal purpose of this book to investigate which of these contentions is the more plausible, and what further implications we should draw from any conclusion we reach. To begin this investigation, it will be valuable to look more closely at the concepts of creation, inspiration, and contemplation, first in the religious, and then in the aesthetic context.

THE DYNAMIC OF RELIGION

In *The Evolution of Religion* Edward Caird writes as follows.

Nothing can be more coarse and repulsive than are many of the superstitious customs of savages; nothing can be more absurd and irrational than most of their ideas as to the constitution of the natural and the spiritual world. No civilized being could possibly look to such a source, either for moral guidance or intellectual light. (Caird 1907: i. 13)

A contemporary audience is likely to feel uncomfortable when anyone else's religion is described in this way, even the religion of peoples and cultures long gone. Yet the possibility of some such judgement seems required by the idea that religion, like science, undergoes development across time. Science fits the Hegelian model easily. What we might call the 'spirit' of science lies in the perpetual desire for a more adequate understanding, a more comprehensive theory than any that has been formulated hitherto. This search is never completed, of course, but the history of science does appear to be the continuous realization of the desire. Its realization reveals an internal relation between the *actual* adequacy of the thing sought, on the one hand, and *our conception* of its adequacy, on the other. A crucially important feature of scientific growth and progress is not just better theory, but an evolving conception of what ought to *count as* a better theory. This creates a dialectical relationship between theory and practice in science. The best theories suggest further investigation by which they can be tested, but in turn techniques of investigation refine the tests that those theories must pass. Religion fits the Hegelian scheme much less readily. To begin with it appears to lack anything of the same dynamism. Whereas science is focused on progress and a future in which established concepts and theories come to be discarded in favour of new and better ones, typically religions are static, concerned with preserving ancient texts and doctrines unchanged. Thus the Christian Reformation was about recovery, not discovery. It sought not advance but return.

This difference between science and religion, though real, does not prevent the concept of development applying to both, however. Religion ought not to be confused with theology, which is an intellectual enterprise within it. The goal of science, we might say, is knowledge, and its motor the twin fears of ignorance and error. The goal of religion is the sacred (or the holy), and its twin fears are idolatry and sacrilege. Religion, in contrast to science, is concerned with more than truth and explanation. It prescribes a way of living, so that theological error and ignorance matter only in so far as they lead us into idolatry or sacrilege. This subsidiary role of the intellect lends religion an internal dynamic different from that of science. The religious quest is not first and foremost a matter of intellectual enquiry, and the genuine seeker need not be (and usually is not) a theological theorist of some kind. Even so, it is still correct to speak of religious engagement with the world as a type of search, and it is this that makes it dynamic. The question then is what drives and constrains the activity of searching.

Idolatry is the worship of false or unfitting objects; sacrilege is the failure to accord holy things the veneration they are due. Accordingly, at the heart of any religious quest is the drive to uncover and venerate the properly sacred. This quest may often occasion a return to sacred texts (or holy writ), but even when it does its purpose is still to secure an advance, the advance to *purer* (or purified) worship. The three concepts of creation, contemplation, and inspiration can be located in the search for such purification.

Creation is fundamental because, at heart, fear of idolatry is anxiety that the objects we worship are a golden calf of our own making, or a human monument with feet of clay (to use images from the Jewish scriptures). The iconoclastic movement of eighth- and ninth-century Christianity, renewed in the Protestant Reformation, and the abhorrence of the figurative in Islam are all expressions of this fear. Though iconodules (the defenders of icons) have arguments upon which they can call, they accept as crucial a distinction between the image and the prototype. Athanasius of Alexandria writing in the fourth century says 'The person who bows to an icon, bows to the king in it' (quoted in Nes 2004: 14), and St John of Damascus, formulating a defence in the eighth century, says 'I do not worship matter; I worship the creator of matter who became matter for my sake' (John of Damascus 726/2003: i. 16–17). In other words, iconodules share with iconoclasts the belief that worship of the merely existing is misplaced. The only proper object of worship is that on which all things (including human beings) depend for their existence. In more modern theological language, there are no beings worthy of worship. Only the *ground* of being is properly regarded as holy.

But what is this 'worship' that can be properly or improperly directed? The answer is a combination of attitude and action. Bowing the knee, standing in silence, solemnizing sacrifice, offering prayer and praise can all be described as acts of worship, and within them we find the second of the three concepts—contemplation, which is to say, rapt attention generated by awe. Contemplation as such, though, falls short of worship. It is not enough to be dumbstruck, or deeply attentive out of curiosity. I can contemplate with loathing, and the repellent can compel a horrid fascination. Worshipful contemplation is *drawn* to the object it contemplates with longing and/or love, and we can mark this difference by locating contemplation within a wider concept—veneration.

Veneration in and of itself is compatible with inactivity, whereas religion is a mode of the practical; it is a way of living and being. Accordingly, the veneration of the sacred must lead those who engage in it to being 'inspired' to live in one way rather than another. In its original sense this means being given breath, and thus according to an ancient way of thinking being given life. 'Inspire' and 'enliven' are still common words, of course, but no one any longer subscribes to this view. *Contra* the ancient world, we now take breathing to be a *sign* of life, not its *cause*, and this might raise a question about what concept of 'spirit' it is still meaningful to employ. At the same time, we need not conclude that words such as inspiration, spirit, spirited, and so on are *merely* figurative. We can still use them to make assertions with a truth value. Perhaps when theatre critics say that an actor gave a spirited performance, their description does derive from an outmoded physiology. Yet we can still ask whether what they say is true or not, just as we can ask, and decide, whether (say) a gift was given in the right or the wrong spirit.

A similar point can be made about the language of 'holy spirit', 'divine inspiration', and so on in a religious context. When the prophet Isaiah says that 'the Spirit of the Lord shall rest upon' the servant born of the house of Jesse, this is amplified as 'the spirit of wisdom and understanding, the spirit of counsel and might, the spirit of knowledge' (Isa. 11: 1–2). Such references to a holy spirit can be separated from the metaphysical theories (outmoded or not) that this is normally thought to require. The 'mechanics' of the relation between inspiration and action can be left on one side. All that is required is the possibility of making truth claims about human actions being motivated by the veneration of the sacred. Of course, not all motivation is inspiration, and there is more to be said about this shortly. At this stage, however, it is sufficient to note that virtually every religion makes a connection between venerating the sacred and being inspired to act, and holds that this is the place where a large part of the importance of religion lies.

If this analysis is correct, the concepts of creation, contemplation, and inspiration can be related as follows. Only divine creation is truly sacred; sacredness calls for contemplative veneration; to venerate the sacred is to be inspired. Religious development both in the individual and culturally over time takes the form of a clearer identification of sacredness leading to a purer form of veneration, and thus to a deeper inspiration. Against this background it is illuminating to see how these same concepts—creation, contemplation, and inspiration—are to be found in an alternative sphere of meaning—Art.

CREATION AND INSPIRATION IN ART

In *The Invention of Art* Larry Shiner observes that

the idea of creation has become so banalized that it is difficult [for us now] to appreciate the reluctance of eighteenth-century critics and philosophers to call artistic activity 'creation'. In the early eighteenth century, the dominant term was still 'invention', and the artisan/artist's activity was still seen as construction. (Shiner 2001: 114)

The principal purpose of Shiner's book is to reveal how the concepts of artisan and artist, which were originally interchangeable, came to be distinguished, and, more significantly, came to have a quite different status as a result of the way in which this distinction was understood. As the status of 'the artist' rose, the status of 'the artisan' fell. At one time it was perfectly correct to speak of the art of a carpenter, weaver, or silversmith. Then people began to differentiate between 'mechanical' arts such as metalworking, watch-making, and engineering, and the 'fine' arts of painting, sculpture, poetry, and music. After a time, the 'fine' was dropped, 'art' was a term no longer used of intricate practical skill that required special mastery, until finally 'the arts' became 'Art'.

Part IV of Shiner's book, which describes the culmination of this process, has the title 'The Apotheosis of Art' and its chapters are headed 'Art as Redemptive Revelation' and 'The Artist: A Sacred Calling'. These are not mere metaphors intended to emphasize the high regard in which Art had come to be held. They reflect a real ambition on the part of artists to give Art something of the function of Religion—and crucial to this 'apotheosis' of art was the concept

of creation. Charles Batteux writing in 1746 could still say: 'The
human spirit cannot properly create . . . . To invent in the arts isn't to
give being to an object, but to recognize where and how it is . . . [T]he
men of genius who dig deepest, discover only what existed before'
(quoted in Shiner 2001: 114). One hundred years later Wordsworth
was describing the artist's imagination as an 'absolute power'. The
contrast is with imagination in the sense of 'fancy'. True artistic
imagination calls into existence new worlds—of sight and sound, as
well as people and events. Thus in the course of 'the invention of
art', artistic 'making' came to be regarded as a form of pure creation
and the artist in that sense a creator *ex nihilo*. 'The genius of creation
and the creations of genius had to be believed in before Art with a
capital A could arise', Jacques Barzun contends (Barzun 1974: 31)
and goes on to observe: 'this title of creator, repeated over 100 years,
finally raised the artist to a unique status' (ibid. 35).

Accompanying this focus on the work of art as an act of creation
comes a conception of aesthetic appreciation as a form of contemplation, and the life of the aesthete as a sort of *vita contemplativa*.
The idea that aesthetic judgement is a distinctive mode of attention
that 'plays freely' on the objects presented to it is of course central
to Kant's account in the *Third Critique*. The Kantian aesthetic has
been immensely influential on the way in which art and the aesthetic
have come to be thought about, and central to it is a concept of
autonomy, which is to say freedom both from causal determination
and from practical usefulness. The slogan 'art for art's sake' is a later
formulation of the same idea. This unique and wholly free judgement
on the part of the art lover, combined with the power of the artist's
imagination to create *ex nihilo* objects worthy of aesthetic contemplation, brings into view a unique and self-constituting world of
experience. Of this world, impressive claims have been made. Louise
Colet enjoined those who participate in it 'Let us love one another
"in Art" as the mystics love one another "in God"' (quoted in
Shiner 2001: 194), and Clive Bell, famous for the doctrine of art
as significant form, remarks that the experience of art so conceived
'might prove the world's salvation' (quoted in ibid. 196).

This spiritual unity of creative artist and contemplative aesthete is achieved through mutual inspiration. The creative spirit or genius of the artist is transmitted to anyone who can and does give serious attention of the right sort, and is thus shared by them. To read Jane Austen attentively is to enter the moral and psychological world that she created and thus in some sense to 'be' in that world with her. To experience the power of Rembrandt's imaginative visions, we have to construct 'The Nightwatch' in our own imaginations. Otherwise it remains simply pigment on canvas. To listen attentively to the music of Beethoven is to be transported into a world of sounds and harmonies in such a way that we participate directly in the imaginative genius of Beethoven. But if such experiences are to be more than subjective diversions, or even emotional 'highs', they must inspire in a fashion something similar to the religious case. Barzun quotes the French novelist Romain Rolland, author of an enormously successful *Life of Beethoven*, first published in 1902, who recalls the experience of hearing Beethoven's symphonies that led him to undertake the biography. 'Alone with the creator, confessing myself to him on the foggy banks of the Rhine ... I went back to Paris with his benediction, restored, having taken a new lease on life and singing a hymn of thanks as from a convalescent to the Deity. That hymn is the present book' (Barzun 1974: 77–8). The emulation of religion could hardly be plainer. The contemplation of artistic creation, like the contemplation of God's creation, must lead to or influence ways of living and being.

ACTION, MOTIVATION, AND INSPIRATION

In the case of art, as in the case of religion, in employing the concept of inspiration we need not make any metaphysically weighty assumptions. Though Rolland's language suggests it, such inspirational experiences as he describes can be explained without deifying artists in the sense of changing their ontological status, or attributing the phenomenon of inspiration to metaphysical causes. A simpler interpretation is available by looking at ways in which people are motivated to act. A longstanding tradition in philosophy (with which Socrates contends at length in the early Platonic dialogues) holds that there is one basic form of motivation, namely self-interested desire, and that all other apparent kinds of motivation must be deduced from or cashed out in terms of it. Among the most famous proponents of this view were Hobbes and Mandeville, and their arguments still find adherents. Nevertheless, as a description of how human beings operate, rational egoism requires a degree of calculative reflection that most people simply do not go in for. Whether at any given moment the task engaged in is the one most likely to maximize self-interest is a question we rarely stop to investigate, or would know how to. Whatever the merits of egoism as a normative standard of practical rationality (an account of how we *ought* to decide what to do), it seems that any attempt simply to summarize and classify human motivations should focus on a less calculative or reflective level. Normally, our motivations to act are more immediate than the assessment of consequences.

These more immediate motivations fall within some very general classifications. People often act as they do just because there is something to be done. 'Something to be done' might be opening up the store, getting the bus to work in the morning, taking the car to be serviced, or keeping a medical appointment. Each of these, though not all 'work' in the strict sense, can be contrasted with leisure, and this brings in a different type of motive. Ordering dinner, planning a holiday, watching television or just chatting are actions that arise from the anticipation of enjoyment, and not because they 'have to be done'. The majority of lives, however, are not completely filled with the actions arising from reasons of work and leisure. For the vast majority of people, an additional, distinguishable motivation lies in caring about others. Listening to a friend in trouble, teaching my daughter to ride a bicycle, or visiting my mother in hospital are all things I have reason to do, not because they have to be done, or will be enjoyable, but because they involve people I care about. Though practical necessity and the prospect of enjoyment can certainly enter into personal relationships, the claims of 'familiars' generally function as an independent source of motivation.

All these are relatively unreflective motivations. We do not usually look for justifying reasons to go to our paid employment, or to watch a television programme we expect to enjoy, or to spend time helping our children with their school work. Rather, these are taken to be foundational reasons, and being motivated by them is accepted as the norm without further justification. Indeed, the request for a justification—Why are you doing what you enjoy doing? Why are you helping those you love?—would in most circumstances be regarded as unintelligible. And, yet, there is a certain mood or cast of mind that leads human beings to ask just what the common round and daily task amounts to, whether everyday life really is worth living, or whether it is just a matter of putting in the time between the cradle and the grave. This mood undermines most easily the reason for doing the things that need to be done. All the ordinary things of life—tidying up the house, going to work, washing the car, arranging insurance—come to seem fruitless and pointless. With equal ease, this same mood can make leisure activities pall. A kind of boredom—*ennui*—saturates everything. Yet more devastatingly, it can even erode personal relationships. In extreme cases, the effort to climb out of this mood leads to their pointless destruction.

Nowadays, when we encounter this mood in ourselves or others, a reductivist tendency inclines us to reach for pathological explanations, of which 'clinical depression' is the most familiar. This is an important mistake in so far as it removes *ennui* from the realms of meaning. It may be true that sometimes lack of motivation is evidence of physiological disorder, but it can also be a manifestation of spiritual malaise. John Kekes has convincingly identified boredom as one of 'the roots of evil' (see chapter 7 of his book of this title). Viewed as a spiritual malaise, it cannot be cured by reaching for the medicine cabinet. But neither can we simply go on appealing to the claims of work, leisure, and family as foundational. We have lost the thing that animates their claim on us, a sense of meaning to our lives. If it is to be restored, we must turn to what I have called 'spheres' of meaning, some larger frame within which we can find renewed enthusiasm for the common round of work, leisure, and family life. One natural way of putting this is to say we are seeking 'something to inspire' us. That is how Art and Religion come to present themselves as alternative, rival, or possibly allied claims on our attention. A person's religion, if not merely conventional, is the ground upon which the meaning and value of their existence rests. Religious faith can inspire to great heights of sacrifice and endeavour (and occasionally great heights of wickedness). More ordinarily, it lends enduring significance to what must otherwise seem ephemeral (a topic to be returned to). Now, as some of the quotations offered earlier make plain, it is incontestable that a number of artists and art theorists have claimed something similar for art, chiefly those who have laid greatest emphasis on the autonomy and self-sufficiency of the world of aesthetic experience. This is an important aspect of the concept of 'Art' that can be seen to have evolved over the two and a half centuries that witnessed (as Shiner expresses it) 'the separation of the artist from the artisan'. It is just such a conception Nietzsche has in mind when he says that 'our highest dignity lies in the meaning of works of art—for it is only as *an aesthetic phenomenon* that existence and the world are eternally *justified* (Nietzsche 1886/1993: 8; emphasis in original).

This last remark introduces the element of rivalry. Barzun, in 'The Rise of Art as Religion', the second of his Mellon Lectures on Fine Art, offers a good deal of evidence that, in the course of the nineteenth century, artists came to have what we might call grandiose spiritual ambitions. 'As early as 1837 we have the revolutionary artist and the transcendental artist fighting side by side. Their voices have rung in chorus ever since, because their common religious task is to repel the world, with or without the zeal to remake it' (Barzun 1974: 38). In support of his view he quotes among others Vincent Van Gogh: 'To try to understand the real significance of what the great artists, the serious masters, tell us in their masterpieces, *that* leads to God' (quoted in ibid. 45). But the words here attributed to Van Gogh might be interpreted more modestly. Such a comment could be made about Caravaggio or J. S. Bach—that their masterpieces were meant to lead to God—and could thus be construed as placing Art in a properly subservient position to Religion. This is precisely its relation for most of its history. What transforms the thought in Van Gogh's remark into the claim of a rival is the relative positions that Barzun attributes to Religion and Art in the wider culture.

[I]t required the Renaissance glorification of man, the scattering and weakening of creeds by the Protestant Reformation, and the general unbelief caused by the progress of science, before art and artists could achieve their present position in the world of intellect. The goal and spur of religion had to be withdrawn from the other world to this world. (Barzun 1974: 33)

The references to the Renaissance and the Reformation are a little misleading since they locate the origins of the apotheosis of art long before Art's claim to be Religion's rival. It was during the eighteenth century that the fine arts distinguished themselves from the mechanical arts, and it was the same century that saw an increasing emphasis on creation and contemplation as central aesthetic concepts. Whether or not the ultimate cause was a 'weakening of creeds by the Protestant reformation', it was in the nineteenth century, over 300 years after Luther nailed his ninety-five theses to the door of the church in Wittenberg, that this change took on its most dramatic significance. For this was when the rise of Art was perceived to coincide with a decline in Religion.

Art raises its head [Nietzsche tells us] where religions decline. It takes over a number of feelings and moods produced by religion, clasps them to its heart, and then itself becomes deeper, more soulful, so that it is able to communicate exaltation and enthusiasm which it could not do before ... Growing enlightenment has shaken the dogmas of religion and generated a thorough mistrust of it; therefore feeling, forced out of the religious sphere by enlightenment, throws itself into art. (Nietzsche 1878/2004: 150)

Nietzsche here sketches a general possibility, but one that he thought had been realized in his own time. It was a belief shared by many others.

There is not a creed which is not shaken, not an accredited dogma which is not shown to be questionable, not a received tradition which does not threaten to dissolve. Our religion has materialized itself in the fact, in the supposed fact; it has attached its emotion to the fact, and now the fact is failing it.... More and more mankind will discover that we have to turn to poetry to interpret life for us, to console us, to sustain us. Without poetry our science will appear incomplete; and most of what now passes with us for religion and philosophy will be replaced by poetry. (Arnold 1880/1964: 235)

This is Matthew Arnold affirming Nietzsche's possibility as both a reality and a *hope*. The affirmation consists of two parts: that the traditional Religion of Europe has failed, and that Art can replace the loss that this failure represents. The remainder of this book consists in an investigation of these two claims.

2

Secularization, Secularism, and Disenchantment

SECULARIZATION

The previous chapter concluded with Nietzsche's contention that 'growing enlightenment has shaken the dogmas of religion'. He wrote this in 1878, four years before he made his memorably dramatic announcement (in *The Gay Science*) that 'God is dead'. In the succeeding century, contrary to what sympathetic readers of Nietzsche have been led to expect, organized Christianity did not disappear. It does seem to be widely agreed, however, that there has nonetheless been a change of great consequence. Whereas the Christian religion once dominated European culture, it has now receded to the margins. This is the phenomenon widely known as 'secularization'. Though the debate about secularization—its nature, extent, and cause—is primarily a subject for historians and sociologists of religion, some discussion is relevant here because of its close connection with a deeper philosophical debate about secularism.

A popular interpretation sees Europe's past as 'Christendom', a lost world in which the Christian religion was inextricably entwined with political and cultural institutions and intellectual ideas. Just how dominant religion really was is not so easy to establish, however. One important question is what is meant by 'dominant'. There have always been atheists and sceptics, and many of them have been significant and influential thinkers. More importantly, perhaps, there have always been scoffers. The expression 'hocus pocus' is of medieval origin, and a mocking distortion of the central words of the Christian mass; in English the holy names of God, Jesus, and Christ are commonly used as expletives; the thirteenth-century poems written by monks that Carl Orff set to music in *Carmina Burana* are deliberately profane. Even in Calvin's Geneva a few people could be found claiming that Jesus was a liar and the Apostles dupes. 'Dominant', then, cannot mean either undisputed or sacrosanct. Conversely, even in contemporary Europe there is no shortage of public and intellectual figures whose adherence to the Christian religion is known and respected (not least, of course, the Pope), and deliberate lampoons or profanations of the life of Christ still meet with vocal protest. Accordingly, the world that has been 'lost' is not without representation or defence in twenty-first century Europe. Moreover, despite post-colonial immigration and the ideology of multiculturalism, if the current status of the Christian religion in contemporary Europe is properly described as 'marginal' it is nevertheless quite different from that of Hinduism, Islam, or New Age.

Nor can the concepts of dominance and marginality be spelt out more fully by the use of statistics relating to churchgoing and other religious practices. One obvious difficulty is that, for a large part of the past, statistics are simply unavailable. In the Victorian period, especially in Britain, figures on church attendance were collected with a fervour and efficiency that has rarely been matched at any other time, and certainly has no counterpart in earlier periods. Such evidence as we can gather about Christian adherence and practice before the Victorian period suggests that this fluctuated. After the powerful and competing enthusiasms of the English Civil War, for instance, in many quarters the Restoration period witnessed a drastic reduction in religious ardour, past the point of scepticism and almost to the point of cynical indifference. Almost a century later, Anglican communicants in the American colonies formed a higher proportion of the population than communicants in the Church of England Diocese of Oxford (see Prichard 1991: ch. 3).

A similar point might be made about numbers of baptisms, weddings, and ordinations. We simply do not have the statistics available to us. Besides, though experts can make educated estimates, mere numbers will not tell us what we want to know. How many vocations to the priesthood or religious orders in times past were more the result of economic circumstances than spiritual calling? The Church and its monastic orders represented one of the most stable and secure forms of employment, as well as the only formal education available, and its hierarchy had a flexibility and openness that the political system did not. Solemnized Christian marriage may have been a spiritual ideal for many, but it also had special importance for family alliances and the orderly transfer of property across generations. Later it was widely encouraged among other classes partly for the purposes of social and political record and control. What do these facts say about its specifically religious significance? These are crucial questions for anyone interested in the religiosity of times past, but not questions that even good statistical evidence could answer. The point is mirrored in this fact. Despite the decline in religious observance of all sorts as evidenced by church statistics, official censuses continue to show that millions of contemporary Europeans think of themselves as Christian, and even that they identify with particular denominations. In social surveys, millions more are calculated to have religious beliefs of some sort.

These remarks about evidence are not meant to rebut the claim that the position of Christianity, and religion more generally, is vastly different now from what it was in times past. To begin with, no evidence from surveys of opinion, however extensive, is likely to displace the shared and firm conviction that twenty-first century Europe is a largely secular society where once it was a largely religious one. But the *nature* of the debate about secularization is as important as the positions espoused within it. 'Secularization' is a thoroughly familiar term and widely used. Does it *explain* the change from a religious to a secular culture, or does it merely describe it? It *sounds* like a process of some kind, but, if it is, when exactly did it begin?

One long-standing contention is that the secularization of Europe has been going on for centuries, and its origins can be traced back to the time when populations began to move in large numbers from countryside to city. Urbanization, it is alleged, destroyed the medieval patterns of life and culture upon which religious life was built. Then industrialization brought increasing wealth and new technologies, loosening the appeal of and dependence upon the quasi-magical methods of religion such as prayers, blessings, and exorcisms. Together, urbanization and industrialization laid the foundations of secularization.

An explanation something like this is widely assumed to be true, and is called upon to explain the significant shift in Christian adherence from north to south. If the churches of Europe are struggling to survive, the churches of sub-Saharan Africa are growing at (probably) unprecedented rates. Since industrialization has hardly touched the countries of Central and Eastern Africa, this is just what the usual explanation of secularization would lead us to expect. The trouble is that it appears to fly in the face of other, equally important evidence. A standing objection to the general thesis, much discussed, is that of the United States, where wealth and technological advancement are found alongside widespread religiosity, often in large cities. If the explanation of secularization relies on the hypothesis that hi-tech urban life is not conducive to religion, how can the United States be one of the most religious nations on earth? There are, of course, many contemporary Americans (especially in universities) to whom this religiosity is alien, but it might be best to classify them (as Karol Berger does) as 'secular children of post-Enlightenment Europe' (Berger 2000: 73), rather than newly secularized Americans.

A further and more recent objection of a similar nature comes from China. Whereas the Chinese Communist Party could declare in 1979 that in one of its major cities—Wengzhou—religion was dead and the city now officially atheist, twenty-four years later 14 per cent of the population of the very same city was estimated to be Christian, most of them 'new' Christians (see Aikman 2004). This is one instance of what appears to be a much wider trend within China as a whole. Following the regime of relative economic freedom inaugurated in 1979, greatly increased urbanization, industrialization, and general prosperity have been accompanied, it appears, by a marked *revival* of religion generally and Christianity in particular. Though prediction is always a precarious matter, it seems quite likely that by 2020 or 2030 the number of new Christians in China will more than offset the declining number in Western Europe.

The 'urbanization and industrialization' explanation of secularization confronts important empirical difficulties, but the case of the United States (and China too perhaps) cannot serve as a straightforward refutation. This is because of yet another dimension to the debate about secularization—namely, its nature. The vitality, like the mortality of religion, has largely been based on statistics relating to church attendance. This ignores the possibility that churches might themselves become secularized, however, so that their vitality is, oddly, evidence of the weakening rather than the persistence of religion. Such a claim has been made quite frequently, and with some plausibility in the light of 'modernist' trends in contemporary mainstream Christian churches. Conversely, the flight from these same churches can bear another interpretation—a move to re-sacralize the world through New Age and other 'spiritual' movements.

In short, the 'evidence' is multiply interpretable, and this makes any straightforward inference from it problematic. Actually, even the European experience presents evidential difficulties for the explanation of religious decline as a consequence of 'modernity'. One of the most open, explicit, and sustained rejections of the Christian religion ever to occur in European history—the French Revolution—took place in a country that was neither urbanized nor industrialized, and where no major technological innovations had changed the pattern of life in the way that the railways, the telephone, and antibiotics did later. And the same conditions applied in the second most striking such episode—the Russian Revolution. By contrast, in the most industrialized countries of Europe—Britain and Germany—no such open rejection of religion occurred.

The case of France suggests an alternative explanation—that
religion fell victim to the impact of Enlightenment philosophy.
While the twentieth century preferred sociological theories that
appeal to material factors, nineteenth-century thinkers were more
inclined to an explanation couched in terms of changing beliefs
and ideas, and a generally accepted philosophy of history developed
around this suggestion. Among its many authors was Auguste Comte,
who, in common with others, divided human history into three broad
divisions—the theological, the metaphysical, and the scientific. This
way of thinking construes secularization not as a sociological process
driven by economic and technological factors, but as a progressive
development in the history of ideas, which then expresses itself
in different social forms. It is plausible to suggest that such an
explanation is overly intellectualist. Only a tiny minority of people
subscribe to religious beliefs as a result of intellectual conviction,
so it does not seem very likely that intellectual uncertainty will be
any more major a factor in generating unbelief. But in any case,
as with sociological explanations, the general picture is difficult
to square with even a relatively cursory glance at the evidence.
While it may be true that, among French Enlightenment thinkers,
philosophy displaced theology, the same is not true of the Scottish
Enlightenment. Hume aside, the most enthusiastic and influential
proponents of a new philosophical 'science of man' were educated
clergy such as Hutcheson and Reid, and even Hume expressed his
admiration for and debt to the Anglican Bishop Butler.

The further element in the Comtean picture—that all this was a
prelude to a truly scientific age—draws support from the undoubted
impact of Darwinian biology on religion. Yet, though this is a
subject to be returned to at several different points, the story of
European Christianity in the nineteenth century does not accord
very easily with the simple suggestion that scientific knowledge
eroded its credibility. The place of the Church in France had already
been eroded. Schleiermacher published *On Religion: Speeches to its
Cultured Despisers* in 1799, an essay addressed to German intellectuals
long before the theory of evolution had had any serious intellectual

impact. In Spain and Italy Catholicism remained secure. In 1799 Schleiermacher regarded the cause of religion in Britain as hopeless as it was in France, yet fifty years later there was something of an explosion of Christian piety, especially in the cities (yet another problem case for the view that urbanization and religion make uneasy bedfellows). So marked was this explosion, in fact, that it has been argued (notably by Callum Brown) that *The Death of Christian Britain* (the title of his book) is a far more recent phenomenon than the familiar theory of secularization suggests. It is also a far more dramatic one, being the result not of a slow erosion over centuries so much as of a sudden collapse within a couple of decades, the outcome of the cultural sea change that was inaugurated in the 'swinging' 1960s.

Some of Brown's evidence for this is a topic to be returned to at a later stage. For present purposes, though, it is worth dwelling on an important observation that he makes. One of the reasons we have such comprehensive statistical evidence from nineteenth-century Britain is that the people who promoted and organized its collection were themselves obsessed with the idea that religion was in decline. Whereas the figures they assembled now incline us to think of the Victorian era as the zenith of Britain's religiosity, contemporaneously this was not how matters were perceived. This is not to say that they possessed statistical evidence from previous periods showing numbers to have dropped. Their concern was driven not by evidence, but by anxiety. They did not *know* that religion was in terminal decline; they *feared* that it was.

Focusing on this fear brings another, and in some ways more manageable dimension to the subject, because it shifts the focus from the descriptive to the normative. The debate about secularization—its nature and explanation—continues to generate a vast literature. In the light of the rise of Islam, and new Christian movements, some recent writers have suggested that, far from being a permanent shift in human mentality, secularization is simply one historical phase now drawing to a close (see Kepel 1991/1994). More importantly, though, the debate about the facts has always been accompanied by debate about their evaluative significance. Is the decline/revival of religion a good or a bad thing? Just as the avid gatherers of statistics feared the decline of religion, others (like Comte in fact) saw in the same prospect a source of liberation—from ignorance, superstition, social conformity, and clericalism. As a result, they gave it an enthusiastic welcome. Both parties shared the belief that a huge cultural change was in view. The subsequent and continuing debate about secularization—its nature, timing, causes, and extent, the uncertainty of the conclusions to be drawn from even a very careful consideration of historical data, and the emergent data from the developing world—means that they may both have been right *or* wrong. But the Victorian debate further shows that it was not ultimately the facts of the case that animated the dispute. At the heart of their debate was a connected, and rather different, issue. Was the emergence of a secular world a change for better or worse? In short, at bottom theirs was a debate not about secularization, so much as about *secularism*.

SECULARISM

The issue at stake in this second debate is a philosophical one. Moreover, without any implausible intellectualism, it can properly be regarded as having its roots in the period of the Enlightenment, which set freedom of thought against ecclesiastical authority and raised the spectre of a conflict between the fundamental doctrines of the Christian religion and the pursuit of rational enquiry. People may or may not come to faith or doubt as a result of reasoning, but, if reason properly understood is logically incompatible with religious belief (as Hume famously alleges in his essay on miracles), a philosophical question arises as to which we ought to favour. On one interpretation, the knowledge that rational enquiry brings means freedom from irrationalism and superstition. On another interpretation, the unrestrained use of human reason is one more manifestation of hubris, and as such destined to undermine any ultimate meaning or purpose. Voltaire is a name commonly associated with the first position, though anti-religion was only part of his radicalism. Hume is another. But among the voices ranged against them were those of respected intellectual figures who could also claim to speak on behalf of reason and rationality. It is simply a mistake to view the discussion of religion in the eighteenth century as a debate between Enlightenment reason and pre-Enlightenment dogmatics. One of the most sustained replies to Hume's essay on miracles was by George Campbell, another Scottish philosopher no less imbued with the intellectual values of the Enlightenment.

Hume's *Dialogues concerning Natural Religion* (published after his death) are often taken to be both an exercise in the critical reasoning characteristic of the Enlightenment and a pivotal point in the history of religion—the point at which the conflict between reason and religion was revealed so sharply that the intellectual credibility of religion began to recede. D. Z. Phillips terms it 'Hume's Legacy' and thinks that its effect is

to make any attempt to infer the existence of God from the world in which we live logically problematic. Its practical effect in the world of nature is to make us treat nature naturally. Similarly, in the world of human affairs, the explanation sought for will be in human terms. Hume's criticisms constitute a powerful attack on the notion of two worlds, an earthly one and a heavenly one, the latter being the explanation of the former. (Phillips 1976: 22)

But, if Hume did leave this legacy, it did not take effect for some considerable time. Twenty years *after* the *Dialogues*, and to great acclaim, Paley published his *Natural Theology*, in which he advanced the very argument that Hume is supposed to have destroyed. Even Hume's own view is a matter of some uncertainty. Philo, the character through whom Hume is generally thought to voice his own opinion, provides apparently insurmountable objections to the argument from design, and yet remarks at the close of the *Dialogues* that 'the beauty and fitness of final causes strike us with such irresistible force, that all objections appear (what I believe they really are) mere cavils and sophisms' (Hume 1779/1947: 214). This is frequently interpreted as being ironic, but it is plausible to hold that Hume was himself a deist of some sort, who objected, not to religion per se, but to *superstitious* religion. Besides, Hume's philosophical writings set sceptical challenges for many moral and metaphysical views and not just for those of Christian theology. He was neither unique nor alone in his religious scepticism, and had no monopoly on the appeal to reason. In short, a common view of Hume's *Dialogues*—that somehow they tipped the intellectual balance in a way that put religion permanently on the defensive—may be reading contemporary concerns into them.

If there was such a pivotal event, it came later, with the advent of Darwinian biology and biblical hermeneutics. An important weakness of attacks (like Hume's) on the 'argument from design' was the absence of any plausible alternative explanation for the perceptible order in nature. This is perhaps why Hume himself, like most of his contemporaries, may have remained unpersuaded by them. But Darwin's account of evolution, if it did not entirely provide it, pointed in the direction of a strictly natural and persuasive alternative—adaptation by means of random mutation and natural selection. At the same time, any claim that the publication of Darwin's *Origin of Species* in 1859 is the turning point for religious belief needs to be stated with care. It does indeed seem that a notable number of nineteenth-century intellectuals faced some sort of crisis with respect to the credibility of both theology and the Bible, that they regarded this crisis as unprecedented in the history of the Christian religion, and that they believed it to have been induced by the results of 'scientific' enquiry, broadly understood. This phenomenon, however, was by no means entirely due to Darwin. In his Gifford Lectures, *The Secularization of the European Mind in the Nineteenth Century*, Owen Chadwick charts a more complex story in which the conflict between science and religion is interwoven with a far older conflict between Protestant individualism and the authoritarianism of the Catholic Church. More tellingly for present purposes, he shows the difficulty of moving from the existence of serious doubt in certain sections of society to any more ambitious inference about the credibility of religious belief in the populations of Europe at large. The decline of religion, when it occurs, is a broad cultural phenomenon not confined to the world of intellectuals, and the relation between intellectual enquiry and popularly held beliefs is a very complex one. The common idea that loss of theoretical credibility among scholars and scientists must sooner or later lead to loss of credibility for popular versions of similar theories in the wider world rests on a naive understanding of this relationship. Chadwick notes how as early as the 1880s an English schoolboy is reported as hearing that 'Darwin has disproved the Bible', so it is certainly the case that the debate and its significance spilled out beyond the confines of the academy. At the same time, Victorian religiosity as measured by church building and attendance actually intensified in the decades after the publication of Darwin's *Origin of Species*.

We could see this increased concern with religion in the wake of Darwin as a sort of death throe, of course. To do so, however, is to introduce an even more complex conception of the relation between intellectual enquiry and social practice. A more promising alternative for present purposes is to regard 'secularization' as itself an intellectual conception of the nineteenth century. At the end of the eighteenth century, Schleiermacher describes a world in which 'the life of cultivated persons is removed from everything that would in the least way resemble religion', people in whose 'tasteful dwellings there are no other household gods than the maxims of the sages and the songs of the poets' (Schleiermacher 1799/1996: 3). What turned the intellectual contempt of an educated minority into the nineteenth-century 'secularization' of society at large was widespread subscription to a philosophy of history according to which human history is (among other things) an embodiment of intellectual progress. Consequently, events in intellectual history are *ipso facto* significant social and cultural events also, and thus the educated elite becomes the cultural vanguard of the rest. As is well known, it was Hegel in his *Lectures on the Philosophy of World History* who gave this conception its most sophisticated formulation, but his was a version of the Christian conception of history we find in Augustine's *City of God*.

Whatever may be true (or have been true) of religious belief and practice in society at large as a matter of empirical fact, this progressive conception of history led those intellectuals who clearly understood the explanatory power of evolutionary theory and could appreciate the implications of historically informed biblical criticism to view these intellectual developments as momentous events for traditional Christianity. They were, of course, events of which vast numbers could remain ignorant, and that others better informed could ignore if they chose. But neither contingent nor deliberate ignorance could escape the fact that these developments had occurred. Scientific discoveries cannot be undiscovered. Their cultural importance, though, cannot be revealed in simple historical or empirical observation and record, because inevitably time has to pass before their significance sinks in. Accordingly, for intellectuals at the time the crucial question was not the immediate impact on church attendance and the like, but the long-term significance for European culture and the meaning of human existence. The statistical surveys they instigated were a way of trying to predict whether and to what extent these new ideas were starting to take hold.

This is precisely the way the matter was viewed by Nietzsche, Christianity's great arch-critic. In sharp contrast to Hume carefully presenting arguments, Nietzsche dramatically announces an event—'the death of God'. In the work where this idea makes its first appearance he writes as follows:

The greatest recent event—that 'God is dead'; that the belief in the Christian God has become unbelievable—is already starting to cast its first shadow over Europe. To those few at least whose eyes—or the suspicion in whose eyes is strong and subtle enough for this spectacle, some kind of sun seems to have set; some old deep trust turned into doubt; to them, our world must appear more autumnal, more mistrustful, stranger, 'older'. But in the main one might say: for many people's comprehension, the event is itself far too great, distant, and out of the way even for its tidings to be thought of as having arrived yet. (Nietzsche 1887/2001: 199)

Such a picture can take full account of continuing, even increased religiosity, as Nietzsche expressly acknowledges.

Christianity, it seems to me, is still needed by most people in old Europe even today; hence it still finds believers. For that is how man is: an article of faith could be refuted to him a thousand times; as long as he needed it, he would consider it 'true' again and again in accordance with the famous 'proof of strength' of which the Bible speaks. (ibid. 347)

But the continuing existence of believers is not of any *ultimate* consequence or significance. If God is indeed dead, the fundamental change whose importance needs to be grasped does not relate to the behaviour of ordinary people, which may for long enough continue in the same old way. Whether they believe or not, their 'belief has become unbelievable' and it cannot any longer have the meaning that they explicitly or implicitly suppose it to have. The issue is how this behaviour is now to be understood and whether it is still *intelligible*. That is why the real debate is not a debate among historians and sociologists about secularization—empirically observable trends in social behaviour—but a debate among philosophers about secularism—whether religion is outmoded as a way in which to live. Furthermore, if God *is* dead, it is not merely *religious* conduct—churchgoing, hymn-singing, prayers for healing, and the like—that is emptied of meaning. The intelligibility of *all* the activity—ethical, political, artistic, educational—that was formed in the light of and took its intellectual nourishment from the theological ideas now exploded is called into question.

It is not his famous contention that 'God is dead' that validates Nietzsche's claim to a major place in intellectual history, but his perception of how far-reaching its ramifications are. This also explains the continuing interest in his writings, despite their extravagant, sometimes chaotic, and occasionally distasteful character. His fundamental insight was that there are ideas and conceptions so central to our understanding of the world that their rejection calls for, and cannot stop short of, 'a revaluation of *all* values', the title of a projected work that the onset of madness prevented him from undertaking. The existence of God is one such idea, and His death, accordingly, calls for just such a revaluation.

We should note, however, several crucial presuppositions. Nietzsche does not argue that God is dead; he takes it for granted, and assumes that there is no way back. Any attempt to resuscitate the central elements in Christian theology—the existence of God, the divinity of Christ, the authority of the Bible, or the equal moral worth of all human beings—is a non-starter. He thus conceives of the revaluation of all values as the central task for a *post*-Christian understanding. Second, he presupposes that such an understanding is possible, that we can adequately revalue all values, albeit with difficulty. In other words, however deep (or broad) the cultural and intellectual crisis induced by the death of God may be, a new and better conception of the significance and meaning of human life can be secured. On Nietzsche's interpretation, Christianity is world rejecting and life denying. Consequently, the death of the God that leads to this denial and rejection holds out the prospect of liberation. Liberated in this way, human beings can become 'free spirits' able once more to relish their lives and their humanity as the ancient Greeks did. But it is not just Christian faith that free spirits abandon. It is the need for *any* faith. In the absence of faith, the free spirit, to use a favourite metaphor of Nietzsche's, finds its expression in an affirmation of the will to dance.

This thought about faith and the will is one to be returned to, though not until the final chapter. The assumption about the intellectual (as opposed to social) resilience of Christianity can be questioned. Some of the most important contributors to Christian theology post-date Nietzsche—Karl Barth, for example—and a sequence of avowedly Christian thinkers, fully appreciating the power of the challenges presented by the intellectual advances of the nineteenth century, have come forward to offer reformulations of Christian fundamentals that take account of those challenges. Of course, Nietzsche, and those persuaded by him, could dismiss all such efforts as inevitably fruitless, but to do so is to retreat to dogma.

We have to enquire whether they are or not. Nietzsche's analysis is insightful and remains challenging, yet, a century and more later, Christian thought, and not just observance, remains part of the intellectual landscape. The second assumption has been less often questioned. Assuming that Christianity does not have the resources for a successful response to secularism, is a revaluation of all values possible that is both humanist and satisfactory? Can we dispense with religious practices and theological presuppositions, and provide an understanding of human existence that makes sense of all the aspects of culture in whose value and importance humanists continue to believe—morality, politics, art? The identification of this issue brings us to the heart of a quite different debate. What is at issue in it is not the truth about secularization but the philosophical adequacy of secularism.

It is important, I think, to disentangle these two debates, though at some level they must be related. There are people (like Nietzsche) for whom the prospect of 'the death of God' is liberating, and it remains so, whether or not the majority continues to give credence to religious beliefs and engage in religious practices. There are other people for whom God's death removes the anchor that secures their deepest moral convictions, and this remains the case even if people go on talking an attenuated language of morality and carry on the business of living in fairly peaceful and orderly ways. Of course, one would expect that, if the idea of God and a divine order really is false and widely said (or assumed) to be so by intellectuals and other opinion-formers, then religious belief and practice would eventually fade away. Conversely, if without theological underpinnings morality is no more than convention and ethics just a kind of etiquette, one would expect the more heroic moral ideas to fall away and the role of positive law as a means of social regulation to grow. The extent to which these changes have come about is an important empirical question, certain to be of great interest to theists and atheists. Nevertheless, the debates about secularism and secularization, though connected, are distinct. It is the debate about secularism with which this book is concerned.

DISENCHANTMENT

In his 1918 speech to Munich University entitled 'Science as a Vocation', Max Weber writes as follows:

Today the routines of everyday life challenge religion. Many old gods ascend from their graves; they are disenchanted and hence take the form of impersonal forces . . . What is hard for modern man, and especially for the younger generation, is to measure up to *workaday* experience . . . The fate of our times is characterized by rationalization and intellectualization and, above all, by the 'disenchantment of the world'. (Weber 1948/2004: 149, 155; emphasis in original)

Weber is writing self-consciously in the shadow of Nietzsche. Two features of his lecture are especially interesting. First, in contrast to Nietzsche, for whom the death of Christianity signals the demise of religion, for Weber it is precisely the end of Christianity (or at least its displacement from centre stage) that has raised again real religious questions. This is because one effect of a thousand years of Christian dominance has been to blind us to what he calls 'the struggles of the old gods'. Second, this blindness was brought about in large part as a result of the powerful emphasis Christianity put on 'the grandiose moral fervour of Christian ethics' (ibid. 149). One important outcome of abandoning this obsession with ethics, is a re-separation between beauty and goodness. 'Since Nietzsche,' Weber says, 'we realize that something can be beautiful, not only in spite of the aspect in which it is not good, but rather in that very aspect.' The importance of Nietzsche's insight in this regard is that it reveals to us again 'the struggle that the gods of the various orders and values are engaged in' (ibid. 148).

Weber's 'disenchantment of the world' is one aspect of what Leszek Kolakowski has called 'The Revenge of the Sacred in the Secular', the title of an essay in his collection *Modernity on Endless Trial*. Kolakowski's thought in this essay, which he describes as 'a suspicion rather than a certainty', is that, though we might suppose it to be liberating, the rejection of the sacred brings a cost with it. Indeed the cost of its rejection might be very high.

Culture, when it loses its sacred sense loses all sense. With the disappearance of the sacred, which imposed limits to the perfection that could be attained by the profane, arises one of the most dangerous illusions of our civilization—the illusion that there are no limits to the changes that human life can undergo, that society is "in principle" an endlessly flexible thing. (Kolakowski 1990: 72)

'Disenchantment' destroys the sense of a culture by reducing the gods to impersonal forces that are incapable of charming or inspiring. Magnetic 'attraction' is not really attraction at all, and music ought to move us in a way different from that in which it moves molecules of air. On Weber's account our world has been disenchanted not simply by the demise of Christianity at the hands of specific discoveries in the natural and historical sciences, but as a result of the attempt to replace Religion with Science as a sphere of meaning, or, more accurately perhaps, the result of the assumption that Science *could* replace Religion in this respect. Moreover, the reduction of the gods to impersonal scientific forces disguises their competition for our loyalties. The presupposition on which the displacement of Religion by Science rests is the idea that Science supplies a principle of rationality capable of determining the merits of every aspect of human existence. But, says Weber, 'I do not know how one might wish to decide "scientifically" the value of French and German culture; for here, too, different gods struggle with one another, now and for all times to come' (Weber 1948/2004: 148).

How is this presumption on the part of Science and its evangelists to be countered? How is the disenchantment of the world to be overcome? Even if we agree that a falsely ambitious conception of Science is importantly impoverishing, and that 'disenchantment' is the right name for this particular impoverishment, can Weber's talk of 'the gods' be anything more than figurative? Is there any serious suggestion here that we might return to pre-Christian ways of thinking? In his revaluation of all values, Nietzsche looks for a return to (some) of the elements of ancient thought that Judaeo-Christianity expunged, but not to their religion. If the God of Judaeo-Christianity is a dying god, all the little gods of Greek and Roman religion or Norse myth are well and truly dead. So what then? Weber is clear that science properly understood opens up no avenue to recovery or re-enchantment, and in the category of 'science' he expressly includes the historical and cultural sciences. These, he says, 'teach us how to understand and interpret political, artistic, and social phenomena in terms of their origins. But they give us no answer to the question, whether the existence of these cultural phenomena has been and is *worth while* (Weber 1948/2004: 145; emphasis in original).

The general point applies, he thinks, even to aesthetics, despite its special concern with the artistic.

The fact that there are works of art is given for aesthetics. It seeks to find out under what conditions this fact exists, but it does not raise the question whether or not the realm of art is perhaps a realm of diabolical grandeur, a realm of this world, and therefore, in its core, hostile to God and, in its innermost aristocratic spirit, hostile to the brotherhood of man. Hence, aesthetics does not ask whether there should be works of art. (ibid. 144)

Should there be works of art? This is a strange question. Whose question is it? We might perhaps rephrase it in a more illuminating way. Does Art enrich the world, and would its loss impoverish it? To most minds the answer to this question is obviously 'yes'. But then there is the further question 'why?'. What is the nature of Art's enrichment of the world? No study of aesthetics that simply accords canonical status to certain pictures, sculptures, pieces of music, literary works, and buildings, and in this sense takes them as 'given', can answer this question. What is required is some account of how the existence of these works makes this a world in which we have reason to *be*. This returns us to the matter of motivation, one of the subjects of the previous chapter. A work of art can give us something to do (restoring it, for example), and works of art are widely regarded (if not always accurately) as objects of enjoyment. Just possibly we might care for them as we do for people (as we sometimes care for heirlooms). But, if they are to motivate at the deepest level, they must inspire. This is what (following Weber) the world revealed by Science cannot ultimately do. The analysis of the previous chapter revealed that inspiration is precisely what Art is often alleged to offer us, and 'inspiring' describes an ambition that has been widely shared by practitioners of the arts.

This is not just a matter of filling a vacuum left by religion. Given the efforts artists made over a long period to disentangle their activities from the cultural history that gave rise to them, and this secure autonomy from the theological doctrines and religious practices that hitherto these activities had served, it is hardly surprising if many artists came to view Art as a new source of spiritual value for a world increasingly uncertain of its religious inheritance. The *spiritual* value of art is central to its having any significant value *as art*.

This ambition is most evident, perhaps, in the Symbolist and Surrealist painters of the late nineteenth and early twentieth centuries, a subject to be returned to at length in the next chapter. But it is also to be found at work in all the major arts—literature, music, and architecture as well as painting. To rest content with recording this ambition and telling the story of its development, however, would be to retreat to what Weber calls a cultural science, not aesthetics so much as the history of art. A wider, and perhaps more compelling interest lies, as he says, in the normative questions that a cultural science does not ask. In 1947, in an essay expressly entitled 'Concerning the Spiritual in Art', the painter Wassily Kandinsky wrote this:

Only just now awakening after years of materialism, our soul is infected with the despair born of unbelief, of lack of purpose and aim. The nightmare of materialism, which turned life into an evil, senseless game, is not yet passed; it still darkens the awakening soul. Only a feeble light glimmers, a tiny point in an immense circle of darkness . . . What is the cry of the artist's soul, if the soul was involved in the creation? 'To send light into the darkness of men's hearts—such is the obligation of the artist' said Schumann. [It is t]he spiritual life to which art belongs, and of which it is one of the mightiest agents. (Kandinsky 1947/1963: 23–7)

Kandinsky's view that a secular world can find in art one of the mightiest agents of its spiritual re-enchantment is the polar opposite of the position argued at length by Jacques Barzun in his Andrew Mellon Lectures:

Art is of all things the worst suited to the purpose. By its very richness and variety art cannot do the simplest things that religion, philosophy and the state can do by *their* nature. In our cant phrase, art cannot be 'a way of life' because—to take examples at random—it lacks a theology or even a popular mythology of its own; it has no bible, no ritual, and no sanctions for behaviour. We are called to enjoy, but we are not enjoined. (Barzun 1974: 90; emphasis in original)

The principal question at issue in this book is who is right about this. Barzun is correct in at least one respect, however. Kandinsky plausibly finds in art an antidote of sorts to materialism, but to show that art can play the role in secular society that religion has done, and continues to do, in pre- and non-secular societies, we have to identify counterparts to several (though perhaps not all) the different aspects of religion—theology, worship, and ethics, for example—which is to say, ideas and beliefs, devotional practices, and prescriptions for the conduct of life. There is no reason to suppose that all these aspects must be reflected in all the arts, and it may be that the different arts supply different aspects that can be woven into a unity. With this possibility in mind, the next four chapters examine the dispute represented here by Kandinsky and Barzun in the specific contexts of painting, music, fiction, and architecture. A concluding chapter will focus on two further art-related concepts—namely, festival and dance. These are concepts to which Nietzsche draws special attention, and their philosophical exploration will provide a more general context in which to offer a concluding assessment of art's ability to assuage 'the revenge of the sacred in the secular'.

3

Seeing the Sacred

THE SCIENCE OF RELIGION

While it seems indisputable that the position of religion in European culture is not what it was, the previous chapter threw considerable doubt on whether the familiar sociological term used to refer to this change—'secularization'—captures any clearly identifiable phenomenon. This is partly because examination of the historical facts is inevitably caught up in a related but different debate about their significance, a debate about the virtues and vices of secularism. The result is that unwarranted assumptions about the facts are as easily made by those who want to 'deal' with secularism in the name of religion as by those who want to trumpet secularism's triumph. So, for example, in *The Sea of Faith*, published in 1984, Don Cupitt repeats the orthodox position without qualification when he asserts: 'The process of secularisation has been going on very slowly for a very long time' (Cupitt 1984: 31). Yet one of the most contentious issues surrounding 'secularization' is the question of timing. Just when did the process begin and when did it come to its height? Other writers, considering the evidence more carefully, have observed that the place of religion in personal life and popular culture remained vigorous in several major European countries long after the advent of those historical developments that Cupitt and others generally assume had undermined it, chiefly Enlightenment philosophy, evolutionary biology, and biblical criticism. Owen Chadwick concludes:

Christians easily reconciled themselves to the general idea of evolution unless they were held from that recognition by dilapidated authorities in their church. When you remember what a revolution this was in men's thinking, and how theoretical much of the construction was and remained, it is extraordinary that it took Europe only about forty years to accept it. (Chadwick 1975: 184)

Our view of the nineteenth-century conflict between Christianity and Darwinian biology, I suspect, is coloured by seeing it through their much later conflict in twentieth-century America, but, in any case, the idea that debates about the intellectual significance of evolution would have had a direct impact on religious belief and practice across society as a whole rests upon a questionable supposition—that ordinary belief is (so to speak) theory driven, that intellectual credibility (or the lack of it) sooner or later determines the popular reception of ideas. It is a supposition that intellectuals make too easily, and often results in a failure to distinguish between intellectual history and the history of beliefs and ideas. It thus assumes that the story of the first—debates between intellectuals regarding the rational acceptability of new ideas—is either identical to, or a precursor of, the story of the latter—the rise and spread of new ideas among populations at large.

This conflation has powerfully influenced the contemporary understanding of secularism and religion. It is widely but falsely supposed that scientific advances were causing popular religious belief to wane in the nineteenth century. The supposition is easily made because it is undoubtedly true that, for a great many nineteenth-century intellectuals, it was these factors that dealt fatal blows to their own religious belief, and alienated them from their Christian inheritance. Those intellectuals could not, of course, make the same mistake about the status of popular religion as succeeding generations have tended to do, since churches, chapels, and meeting places were springing up in large numbers, and great crowds went on attending the major religious festivals. But they explained this continuing respectability of Christianity in public and personal life by concluding that for most people the profound significance they saw in these intellectual developments had not yet sunk in.

Thus Nietzsche's madman, who (in *The Gay Science*) famously pronounces 'the Death of God', also concludes 'I come too early. My time is not yet, this tremendous event is still on its way' (Nietzsche 1887/2001: 120). Twenty years earlier Matthew Arnold had already heard the 'melancholy long withdrawing roar' of faith receding on 'Dover Beach', but Arnold too saw himself as a prophetic voice. The passage quoted in Chapter 1 is worth repeating in this context.

The future of poetry is immense, because in poetry, where it is worthy of its high destinies, our race as time goes on, will find an ever surer and surer stay. There is not a creed which is not shaken, not an accredited dogma which is not shown to be questionable, not a received tradition which does not threaten to dissolve. Our religion has materialized itself in the fact, in the supposed fact; it has attached its emotion to the fact, and now the fact is failing it [under the onslaught of scientific and historical enquiry, presumably]. But for poetry the idea is everything; the rest is a world of illusion, of divine illusion. Poetry attaches its emotion to the idea; the idea is the fact. The strongest part of our religion today is its unconscious poetry. (Arnold 1880/1964: 235)

One striking feature of the intellectuals' self-perception lay in the sense of crisis that it generated; intellectuals felt the loss of a religious foundation very keenly. A hundred years later Europe's cultural elite had come to regard the decline or demise of religion without anxiety, as they often do nowadays, and sometimes even with glee. The outcome is two different sorts of atheism. This is a contrast neatly captured by Graham Greene's novel *Stamboul Train*, in an interesting encounter between Dr Czinner, a Socialist doctor who has abandoned the Catholicism in which he was brought up, and Coral Musker, the heroine, to whom religion means nothing. For both, of course, there is no God, but this fact matters to Czinner in a way it does not and cannot matter to Carol. Following their conversation in the railway compartment, Czinner reflects that

he had blown that candle out with his own breath, telling himself that God was a fiction invented by the rich to keep the poor content; he had blown it out with a gesture, with a curious old-fashioned sense of daring, and he sometimes felt an unreasoning resentment against those who nowadays were born without religious sense and able to laugh at the seriousness of the nineteenth century iconoclast. (Greene 1992: 100)

This difference of mentality, of course, might be regarded as merely a matter of psychological history. But Nietzsche, for whom the 'Death of God' was a most welcome event, was under no illusion about the depth of its implications, or the difficulty of accepting them fully. Certainly, any naive belief that 'science' can simply replace 'religion' and everything proceed as before but more rationally is wholly unwarranted and inadequate to the occasion.

It is still a *metaphysical faith* upon which our faith in science rests—that even we knowers of today, we godless anti-metaphysicians, still take *our* fire, too, from the flame lit by the thousand-year old faith, the Christian faith that was also Plato's faith . . . that truth is divine. (Nietzsche 1887/2001: 201)

Religion, then, even in its death throes, was of enormous importance to the post-Darwinian atheists of the nineteenth century. The sea of faith had not receded to the confines of an individual pastime and personal eccentricity, as it has in the minds of many secularists now. One interesting outcome of this somewhat ambivalent attitude to religion by those persuaded of its intellectual untenability was the emergence of 'the science of religion'. This development provided for a continuing interest in the phenomena of religion, but it did so with the detachment of the observer rather than the attachment of the adherent. Yet, though firmly focused on religion because of a belief in its human significance, the science of religion also contributed importantly to the disenchantment of the world.

Among the figures usually included in the list of those who were major contributors to this development are the Hebraist William Robertson Smith, whose articles on the Pentateuch in the *Encyclopedia Britannica* led to his expulsion from the Free Church of Scotland College in Aberdeen, and Sir James Frazer, famous for his studies in *The Golden Bough*, widely regarded as a seminal text in the anthropological study of religion. Both in their different ways contributed to undermining the special status of the Christian religion. Robertson Smith's investigations in 'Higher criticism' were held to undermine belief in the inspiration of Scripture because, by identifying a number of sources out of which the books of the Old Testament were compiled, they appeared to reduce Holy Writ to ancient literature like any other. Frazer's work was based upon existing documents rather than original fieldwork, and at one level he was simply collating what had been in the public realm for a long time. But he brought this material together so as to reveal parallels between Christianity and primitive religions that were found to be deeply disconcerting. The 'sacrifice of the human god' in Aztec religion, for example, which fell roughly at Easter, was 'found to correspond in date as well as character to the Christian festival of the death and resurrection of the Redeemer' (Frazer 1922/1957: 769). Frazer, in the preface to his abridgement of the full twelve-volume study, declares that the central mythology he studied was one 'which I look upon not merely as false but as preposterous and absurd' (ibid. vii). But to many of his readers the question naturally arose as to why seemingly similar practices should be regarded as 'preposterous' when Christianity was not.

There is a case to be made for thinking that these developments in the 'science of religion' were more powerfully corrosive of Christian belief than the developments in the biological and physical sciences upon which far more attention has focused. In part this was because, by finding the same religious motifs scattered across the whole of human experience, they were perceived to undermine Christianity's claims to uniqueness. However, almost as importantly, they also provided alternative spiritual possibilities for those to whom Christianity had grown stale. Viewed in this way, the revelations of the 'science of religion' provided materials that, in prospect at any rate, might serve to re-enchant the world.

A notable event in this connection was the establishment in 1875 of the Theosophical Society. Founded by Colonel Olcott and the enigmatic Madame Blavatsky, its President subsequently was the famous Mrs Annie Besant. Subscription to theosophy—the belief that all religions contain or reflect the same fundamental spiritual truths—can be found at far earlier periods, but the combination of uncertainty about Christianity together with increasing knowledge of other religions gave it a special appeal at the end of the nineteenth century. The relatively rapid growth of the Theosophical Society is evidence of this appeal, but so too is the extraordinary interest that was shown in spiritualism. Once again, this was not something new; spiritualism is mentioned, and condemned, in the New Testament. But the nature of the interest in it was novel. It led to the creation of the British Society for Psychical Research in 1882, perhaps the clearest institutional example of the 'science of religion'. Its purpose was to investigate the phenomena of spiritualism scientifically, not with a view to explaining them away, but with a view to testing their validity. The aim, we might say, was a scientific assessment of their spiritual or religious worth.

Theosophy and Spiritualism can be thought of as attempting, in their different ways, to rescue religion by giving some of its varieties a 'scientific' credibility that Christianity was held to lack, or to have lost. Interpreted in this way, the aim of both was to square the undeniable supremacy of scientific thinking with the continuing religious interest (and yearning) of sophisticated Europeans—theosophy by identifying something like universally applicable laws, spiritualism by gathering data of the sort approved by empirical science. It is understandable that some people should have regarded this as an attempt to square the circle, and consequently sought an alternative. Their solution was not to shun, but to embrace religion precisely for its *un*scientific character, and to claim for it a region of its own. This was the region of the illogical. It can be characterized in different ways—feeling rather than reason, mystery rather than science, the uncanny and unpredictable rather than the explicable and the predictable.

THE EMERGENCE OF THE SURREAL

Such a response to the steady march of science chimed well with (or perhaps was part of) Romanticism in the arts. Whereas 'taste' and its education are the principal aesthetic concepts of the eighteenth century, in the nineteenth inspiration and expression held pride of place. We find this important change reflected in all the principal arts. Compare Jane Austen's *Emma* with Emily Brontë's *Wuthering Heights*, Bach's *Art of Fugue* with Mahler's *Songs of a Wayfarer*, Gainsborough's 'conversation pieces' with Dante Gabrielli Rossetti's 'romantic medievalism', or Gray's 'Elegy' with Wordsworth's 'Prelude'. These are among the more famous examples of a general contrast that is to be found not just in the arts, but more widely in the world of ideas.

Romanticism lays greatest store by powerful feeling—both experiencing it and expressing it. Accordingly, the mark of artistic genius is twofold—a heightened ability to feel and the mastery of the means by which to express this feeling. The criterion of creative merit is authenticity—the sincere expression of feeling—and the measure of artistic success is the extent to which an emotional response is elicited from the audience or readership. This emphasis upon emotion leads Romanticism, in its most extreme forms, to *rejoice* in illogicality. Once reason is viewed as the ally of prudence, and prudence the enemy of passion; the passion that is most to be admired is that which defies not merely the conventional but the prudential.

It is easy to see how this dual emphasis on feeling and authenticity makes Romanticism in the arts a natural ally of any religion that has come under rationalist attack, and especially the variety of Protestant Christianity that lays great store by religious feeling. The kind of evangelicalism that found its most dramatic manifestations in the American Great Awakenings identified 'the religious affections' rather than metaphysical theory or theological doctrine as the heart of religion, and looked to personal faith rather than doctrinal belief. The rationalist's charge is that religion makes no sense. The emotivist's reply is that religion is a matter of *feeling*, which is about not sense but experience (though in his sermons on *The Religious Affections* (1746) the great American theologian Jonathan Edwards aimed to avoid just such a simplification). Pascal's famous aphorism—'the heart has its reasons which reason does not know'—though coined in a religious context, is readily endorsable by Romanticists.

This common emphasis on feeling, however, does not guarantee that Romanticism's alliance is with Christianity exclusively, or even especially. Once the essence of religion is identified with emotion, the doctrines that distinguish one religion from another lose most of their importance. Indeed, insofar as they set up obstacles in the way of experiencing real religious emotion, they are to be discarded. The result was that Romantics could take up the arcane material produced by the science of religion, and they often did so more enthusiastically than they did the familiar, well-worn Christian images and stories.

One instance of this is particularly striking—the relation between Max Müller, a pioneer of 'the science of religion', and Gerard de Nerval, a major influence in Symbolist poetry. Müller's investigations into the origins of religion (which he found in the *Rig Veda*) resulted both in translations of sacred Eastern texts and in his monumental *Comparative Mythology* (1857). Nerval's poetry artistically transformed this material into mystical visions. The example is one illustrative of a general trend. As Celia Rabinovitch observes: 'The pursuit of the origins of culture combined the scholar's methods of the science of religion with the poet's desire for revelation' (Rabinovitch 2004: 69).

The adoption and adaptation of mythological material on the part of painters, writers, and composers is not one of passive acquisition alone, however. The towering figure in nineteenth-century Romantic art is Wagner, and Wagner recovered for himself the material with which he worked—the mythical stories of medieval Germany and Iceland. Indeed, the anthropologist Claude Lévi-Strauss later credited Wagner with making the huge intellectual advance constituted by the discovery of 'myth' properly so called. Wagner can be said to constitute a major moment in a cultural movement of very considerable importance—the rediscovery of the primitive, the magical, the mythical, the subconscious—as a source of artistic materials. He was by no means alone. Thirty years after Wagner created his opera *Tristan and Isolde* out of Gottfried von Strassburg's thirteenth-century story, the Irish poet W. B. Yeats (another artist who felt deprived of Christianity by evolutionary biology and Higher Criticism) founded the Dublin Hermetic Society for the exploration of Irish folklore with an eye to mining it for poetic and dramatic materials. And a similar rediscovery of the mythical past is evident in Pre-Raphaelite painters who depicted contemporary models as idealized medieval figures, Rossetti's *Beata Beatrix* being paradigmatic.

This artistic interest in the mythical combined with the perception that established religion was in decline gave rise naturally, if not inevitably, to the idea that art might fill the vacuum religion was leaving behind. As noted earlier, Matthew Arnold, commenting some years later on his own observation that 'the strongest part of our religion today is its unconscious poetry', goes on to write

More and more mankind will discover that we have to turn to poetry to interpret life for us, to console us, to sustain it. Without poetry, our science will appear incomplete; and most of what now passes with us for religion and philosophy will be replaced by poetry. (Arnold 1880/1964: 235)

The future Arnold here predicts for poetry was echoed in the other arts. In the almanac of the revolutionary group of artists known as *Der blaue Reiter*, Franz Marc (1880–1916) wrote that true artists were striving 'to create in their work symbols of their time that will belong on the altars of the coming spiritual religion behind which the technical aspects will disappear' (quoted in Rookmaaker 1970/1994: 111). Another member of the same group, the Russian painter Wassily Kandinsky (1866–1944), expanded on this theme in the essay mentioned previously—'Concerning the Spiritual in Art and Painting in Particular'—and in his quest he initiated the hugely influential movement to abstract art. The Dutch painter Piet Mondrian (1872–1944) took the same view of painting and the spiritual, and, after a brief experiment with Cubism, also moved in the direction of abstraction. Commenting on this movement, the art historian H. R. Rookmaaker remarked that, while 'Mondrian and others were building a beautiful fortress for spiritual humanity, very rational, very formal . . . they did so on the edge of a deep, deep abyss, one into which they did not dare to look' (Rookmaaker 1970/1994: 143). But, according to Rookmaaker, another school emerged that did look into the abyss—the Surrealists.

Certainly, it is in the strange and compelling paintings and exhibits of the later Surrealists that we find the most explicit attempt in the visual arts to reveal the irrational, chaotic, and daemonic forces underlying the surface appearance of ordinary life by depicting the weird and the uncanny. The Surrealists' immediate precursors include the Greek painter Giorgio de Chirico (1888–1978). De Chirico's unusually long life encompassed so many movements in the history of modern art that his influence on it, and even his place within it, is a matter of some dispute. But it seems clear that the series of paintings he produced in the period 1911–18, together with a series of *Meditations* he wrote to a friend at the same time, were of very considerable interest to the founders of the Surrealist movement. They are in any case of great interest in the present context, not least because in one of these letters de Chirico expressly connects his paintings with reading Nietzsche for the first time.

De Chirico's self-portrait of 1913 is significantly subtitled 'And what shall I Worship Save the Enigma?' Several of his other paintings have similar titles—*The Enigma of a Day* (1914), *The Mystery and Melancholy of a Street* (1914), and *The Disquieting Muses* (1916). These titles reveal the whole purpose of de Chirico's paintings in this period—the portrayal of the enigmatic, the mysterious, the disturbingly strange in the midst of the ordinary. In *The Mystery and Melancholy of a Street* late afternoon light partially illuminates the figure of a small girl rolling a hoop through an empty street towards a sinister shadow, the source of which is hidden. The precision of the figure and the buildings, combined with the intense colour and deep shading of the scene, creates a powerful and unmistakable impression of foreboding, repeated in several other works. De Chirico's own comment on this painting identifies its central motif as a 'presentiment' that has existed since prehistory. 'We might consider it', he says, 'as an eternal proof of the irrationality of the universe. Prehistoric man must have wandered through a world full of uncanny signs. He must have trembled at each step' (quoted in Rabinovitch 2004: 153). The purpose of his paintings, accordingly, is to recover for us now that sense of the uncanny, to reveal once more the mystery of things as they are.

It is easy to see how this idea of art as the revelation of the inexplicable in the midst of the explicable should appeal to artists in an age when 'science' had largely dispelled mystery at the same time as traditional religion had proved a powerless counter to this 'scientific' domination. And, indeed, this role as the revealer and champion of the mysterious or the irrational is precisely the foundation of Surrealism. Today, it is generally identified as a movement within the visual arts, but its origins actually lay in literature and theatre, where the word was coined by Guillaume Apollinaire, the French writer to whom de Chirico sent his *Meditations*. The subtitle of Apollinaire's play *Les Mamelles de Tirésias* is 'a Surrealist drama'. The term was taken up in a first *Manifest du Surrealism*, which appeared in 1924, and it too was the work of a writer, André Breton. With this manifesto, Surrealism became an artistic movement. Its first members were writers, and their ambition was to break beyond the rational and the ordered by means of 'free' writing (which Yeats under the influence of his wife also explored), the literary equivalent of free association, one of the techniques by which Freud claimed to be able to uncover the irrational forces of the unconscious that lay beneath the conscious mind.

It was not long before visual artists joined the writers, and for a variety of reasons it was the visual arts that came to dominate the movement. Whereas its writers and playwrights are now largely unknown, the figures of Juan Miró, Max Ernst, René Magritte, and, especially, Salvador Dali are and will remain major figures in twentieth-century visual art. The history of visual art since the mid-nineteenth century is the story of a rapid sequence of movements that arose in the struggle to find a distinctive role that would capture and vindicate both the value of art and its autonomy—the Pre-Raphaelites, the Impressionists, the Cubists, and so on. But of all these movements, it is most plausible to see the Surrealists (and to some extent their American successors the Abstract Expressionists) as self-consciously engaged in a sustained attempt to do what Arnold expected poetry to do—namely, to re-enchant a world that had been de-sacralized by science.

SEEING THE SACRED

For present purposes it is not enough to record that this was indeed their ambition. The more interesting, indeed crucial, philosophical question is the extent to which they succeeded. Judged simply as visual art, the paintings of the principal Surrealists show an outstanding mastery of their medium. It is a common complaint that 'modern art' (in its loosest connotation) makes little use of the techniques slowly acquired in the course of the history of painting. Indeed, so completely have these been abandoned that it is common to hear the allegation that 'anyone' could paint a modern work, since neither skill nor knowledge is required. While perhaps this complaint can be brought with justice against some of the abstract, pop, and conceptual art of the last hundred years, it could never be plausibly levelled at the work of Max Ernst, René Magritte, or Salvador Dali. Each of them exhibits an astonishing facility with depiction, colour, and perspective.

Abstract painters such as Kandinsky and Mondrian discarded representative painting in order not to be distracted from the spiritual by the identifying appearance of things. Surrealist painting, by contrast, retained the techniques of realistic representation precisely in order to reveal the deep incoherence in these appearances. René Magritte's *The Listening Chamber* (1953), for example, shows a huge apple filling the room of an ordinary suburban house. The gross incongruity of the object and the space it occupies requires that both be depicted with great representational accuracy. Otherwise it would not work. Similarly, the 'shock' value of Max Ernst's grotesque *The Robing of the Bride* (1940) requires that the fantastic figures in it are clearly depicted and precisely arranged. And, even if there is little by way of accurate depiction in Miró, a picture such as *Head of a Woman* (1938) reveals an impressive control over colour and composition.

On seeing *Metamorphosis of Narcissus* (1937), Freud expressly commented on Dali's technical mastery. But, in common with that of the other Surrealists, Dali's accomplishment is not technical in a narrow sense. The art of the painter differs from that of the illustrator, and part of the difference lies in the fact that a painting's purpose is to do more than merely present a visual image for the viewers' inspection and information. While it is the mark of a good illustration that it aids recognition, a great painting commands and directs our perception. In *Metamorphosis* (as in many of Dali's paintings) we are compelled to see a visual parallel between animate and inanimate. The figure of Narcissus is transformed once we have looked at the stone pillar that mirrors him, and back again. So too in the famous *Swans into Elephants*, the inanimate reflection of swans in the water takes on the animate reality of elephants.

The Surrealists, then, are continuous with the tradition of Western art in a way that most other movements in 'modern' art are not. In another respect they also differ—namely, popular reception. Of all the many movements in twentieth-century visual art, Surrealism has probably had the greatest popular appeal. Some of this is due to the impressive skill so many of the paintings exhibit. Another important factor was Salvador Dali's hugely successful self-promotion, especially in America, an enterprise in which he was assisted by his wife, Gala, who managed its financial aspects. Other Surrealists disapproved—André Breton made an anagram of his name, 'Avida Dollars'—but the movement as a whole benefited greatly from the attention it brought. A similar factor was the influence of the collector Peggy Guggenheim, who was married to Max Ernst for a brief period (1942–6). A fourth factor, and more significant for present purposes, was Surrealism's connection with the cultural context of its times, one in which Freudianism figured prominently. Dali himself was an admirer of Freud, whom he met in 1938 in London, and the connection was made known to a very wide public by Dali's pictures for the dream sequence in Alfred Hitchcock's 1945 film *Spellbound*.

The Surrealists were attracted by Freud's theory of the unconscious, and his attempts to access the deepest level of mental life through the interpretation of dreams. Fifty years or more after the decline of Freudianism, it can be difficult to appreciate the immense cultural presence it once enjoyed. The power of its appeal derived from a combination of the age-old human desire to penetrate the surface appearance of things to the secret reality beneath, and the 'forbidden' allure of sex and sexuality suitably covered with the respectability of science. What made it especially attractive to the Surrealists, despite its supposedly 'scientific' character, was the idea that order is merely on the surface. Underneath lie irrational forces waiting to be revealed. The revelatory nature of the dream world was particularly alluring. Breton, author of the 1924 *Manifesto of Surrealism*, expressly mentions 'the omnipotence of dream'. It is a recurrent theme. Yet the dream world is only one possible source of the strange and illogical. If, as Breton also asserts, the central 'philosophy' of Surrealism is a 'belief in the superior forms of certain forms of previously neglected associations' (quoted in Rabinovitch 2004: 120), the dream is only one such form.

The mark of all these forms of association is their irrationality. In the same *Manifesto*, Breton describes the productions of Surrealism as 'dictated by thought in the absence of any control exercised by reason, exempt from any aesthetic or moral concern' (quoted in Rabinovitch 2004: 120). Once more this is a repeated theme. Paul Delvaux, whose *Dawn over the City* is amongst the best known of surrealist paintings, defines Surrealism as 'the reintroduction of the subject but in a very particular sense, that of the strange and illogical' (quoted in Klingsöhr-Leroy 2004: 46). Max Ernst commends collage on the grounds that it involves 'the magisterial eruption of the irrational in all domains of art' (quoted in Bradley 1997: 27).

This rejection of reason, and especially scientific reason, was just one of the cultural consequences of the First World War. The colossal and pointless carnage in this war, whose sheer scale only slowly became apparent, shocked and stunned most people, of course. But by many intellectuals it was also regarded as a kind of *reductio ad absurdum* of any attempt to govern the world through science and reason. Ernst, who was conscripted to the German army, later wrote in his autobiography 'Max Ernst died on 1 August 1914. He was resuscitated on 11 November 1918, as a young man aspiring to become a magician and to find the myths of his time' (quoted in Bradley 1997: 11).

This sentence provides us with an even better statement of Surrealism's ambition than Breton's self-conscious manifesto—to find the myths of the time—and it brings us back to the question of success. In terms of their own ambition, technical mastery, visual impact, and popular acknowledgement were not enough. The aim was creative revelation—the use of artistic creativity to reveal the secret or hidden nature of things. This ambition was twofold, since the discovery of new myths would at the same time be the displacement of the old. The point gets its most striking visual expression in Ernst's own picture *The Virgin Mary Spanking the Infant Jesus before Three Witnesses* (1926), the witnesses being Ernst himself and his fellow Surrealists Breton and Eluard. The picture uses all Ernst's mastery of figuration, perspective, and colour to show the Virgin Mary in a style that is reminiscent of the high Renaissance while in a posture characteristic of pagan figures, with the infant Jesus across her knee, his halo tumbling to the ground.

But where and how was the material for an alternative myth to be found? In this respect, the Surrealists proved more eclectic than syncretist. That is to say, their unifying idea—the revelation of disturbing incongruities—proved compatible with a very wide disparity in style and content. In several of his paintings Ernst draws upon pre- and non-Christian sources. *Chemical Nuptials* painted in 1948 is a visual version of the esoteric Rosicrucian text *Chemical Wedding*, and in what is probably his most famous painting, *The Elephant of Celebes* (1921), interpreters have found allusions to Greek myth. The women portrayed in Paul Delvaux's *The Break of Day* are versions of Hindu *yakshini*—spirit personifications of trees—and in *Sleeping Venus* of 1944 he makes extensive use of figures portrayed on the walls of the Roman Villa of Mysteries and dating from about fifty years before Christ. Juan Miró also turned to prehistory through the writings of French anthropologist Lucien Lévy-Bruhl, and expressly tells us that 'when I make a large female sex image it is for me a goddess', something his *Head of Woman* amply demonstrates.

Those Surrealists who turned, not to past ideas, but to Freudianism, the most prominent intellectual development of their time, produced an abundance of dream pictures. These compelling works aimed to depict the strange world of the unconscious, though, as Freud himself remarked, however dreamlike, such pictures are products of the conscious, not the unconscious mind. Dali is the most notably Freudian of the Surrealists, his lengthily entitled *Dream Caused by the Flight of a Bee around a Pomegranate a Second before Waking up* being a typical example. But he is not the only one. 'The Key to Dreams' is a whole series by Magritte, whose 1928 work *The Reckless Sleeper* is also replete with Freudian symbols. The title of Yves Tanguy's 1927 *Mama, Papa is Wounded* places it firmly in the same category. *The Colour of my Dreams* is a picture by Miró.

The return to ancient mythologies and the recourse to Freud, with his emphasis on the dream world and the unconscious, are both somewhat at odds with another aspect of Surrealism's aims, which is to reveal the strange and irrational in the world of ordinary, everyday experience. This leads to a third kind of content. Like Dali's dream scenes, Miró's *The Tilled Field* (1923/4) is strange and colourful, but its purpose is to invest features of the familiar Catalan countryside—a horse, a farmhouse, a cactus—with symbolic character and quasi-magical value. Magritte's *The Empire of Lights* (1953/4) looks very different, since it is 'realist' rather than Symbolist in style. But precisely because its depictions of day and night are so convincing, it too gives a Surrealistic feel to a scene from everyday life by putting them both in the same picture. For the most part, this is what Surrealist *objects* do. Dali's 'lobster telephone' creates its weird effect by simply replacing the telephone receiver with a lobster, and Meret Oppenheim's *Fur Breakfast* takes the form of a standard cup, saucer, and spoon made out of materials standardly used for hats and gloves. Man Ray's *Gift* is an ordinary smoothing iron, the flat surface of which is studded with ordinary nails. This is the aspect Surrealist visual art most obviously shares with Surrealist theatre, one of whose major playwrights, Eugène Ionesco, expressly says: 'The surreal is there within our reach, in our daily conversation' (quoted in Styan 1981: 139).

For the most part, it is Magritte's paintings that are spectacularly good at creating dramatic incongruities by means of highly realistic depiction. Their effect is to generate a sense of forcing gaps in the veil of experience through which we are fleetingly allowed to peer. One of the most striking instances, also an example of Magritte's astonishing mastery of the medium, is *Carte Blanche*. A woman is shown mounted on a horse riding in the woods, but the combined figure of horse and woman is, so to speak, woven in among the trees—some parts in front, other parts behind—as though in reality the whole scene is nothing more than a backcloth that might be differently arranged. 'Lift not the painted veil which those who live call Life' is the opening line of a poem by Shelley. Lifting the painted veil seems precisely what Magritte has done.

This considerable variety—ancient mythology, the unconscious, the incongruity of the everyday—presents something of a problem in so far as we understand Surrealism as an attempt to re-enchant the world. With which of these is it to be re-enchanted? A Surrealist might reply that there is no ultimate conflict. As Miró's vast number of works demonstrates, any and all of these, and more besides perhaps, can serve as simply different ways of 'lifting the painted veil'. If so, however, there is this further question. What are we supposed to do, once it is lifted?

ASCETICISM VERSUS MYSTICISM

The problem lies in forging a connection between contemplation and inspiration. How might the contemplation of these glimpses behind the veil motivate action? How could they be construed as relating to ways in which we might live? In his essay 'Art, Religion and the Elite', Nicholas Wolterstorff reflects on a passage from André Malraux's *The Voices of Silence* that draws a parallel between religion and art along similar lines to those we have been examining, and he wants to connect this parallel with the distinction Weber draws between two types of religion—'asceticism' and 'mysticism'. Both arise from a profound dissatisfaction with the world of ordinary human experience, and an unwillingness to affirm it. In both cases the source of this dissatisfaction lies in a sense of the ultimate worthlessness of the world, sometimes because of its meaninglessness, sometimes because of the omnipresence of evil. But the two types differ in their respective responses to this dissatisfaction. The ascetic (by Weber's account) refuses to accept the world as it is, but battles to transform it. The mystic, by contrast, seeks only to fly from it.

From the standpoint of a contemplative mystic, the ascetic appears, by virtue of his transcendental self-maceration and struggles, and especially by virtue of his ascetically rationalised conduct within the world, to be forever involved in all the burdens of created things . . . The ascetic is therefore regarded as permanently alienated from unity with god, and as forced into contradictions and compromises that are alien to salvation. But from the converse standpoint of the ascetic, the contemplative mystic appears not to be thinking of god, the enhancement of his kingdom and glory, or the fulfilment of his will, but rather to be thinking exclusively about himself. Therefore the mystic lives in everlasting inconsistency, since by the very fact that he is alive he must inevitably provide for the maintenance of his own life. (Weber quoted in Wolterstorff 1985: 270)

It should be obvious, Wolterstorff goes on to say,

that the religion of art described by Malraux is structurally akin to Weber's *mystical* religion. There is no god whose obedient instrument one is called to be. There is no ethical struggle to suffuse the world with the actions of obedience in a way that would sacralise one's ordinary experience. The dynamics are all the opposite. One departs from the ordinary world, and by way of contemplation one seeks to come into touch with something higher, better and nobler. (Woltersdorff 1985: 270)

This parallel, however, seems to reflect the visual arts of the eighteenth and nineteenth centuries, before the advent of the modern, and before, therefore, art set itself to occupy the place of religion. To employ Rookmaaker's distinction again, contemplation of something higher, better, and nobler seems to capture the aspiration of art as the 'beautiful fortress for spiritual humanity', an aspiration that some modern artists have shared. But it hardly fits the Surrealists, who dared to look into the 'deep, deep abyss'. 'For them,' Rookmaaker observes, 'fear, agony, despair and absurdity were the real realities. It was these they wanted to take up and express in their art.' Far from putting us in touch with 'something higher, better, nobler',

their works were . . . full of irrationality, absurdity, alienation, sadism, evil and hell, the horrific, black humour. The basic motifs of their work were man's *echec*, his failure to gain true freedom and true humanity, the fact that he is a stranger in this absurd reality that he experiences as a prison, as frustration, as an obstacle in his way through to himself. [And while] surrealism was a movement . . . as such . . . confined and restricted . . . its influence has been great, and it has pervaded much of the expression of our age. Almost all artistic activity since that time has had some sort of surrealistic tinge. (Rookmaaker 1970/1994: 142–3)

Whatever 'modern' art of this kind has to offer, it can hardly be that relief from involvement in 'all the burdens of created things' that motivates the mystic's flight from the world. Modern visual art in most of its manifestations has sought to point us to levels of absurdity that scarcely bear contemplation. If, nonetheless, it requires us to contemplate the realities it depicts, it must equally point out some way of living with the absurdity.

One such way might be simple distraction. Rookmaaker quotes the British painter Francis Bacon to this effect—'painting has become—all art has become—a game by which man distracts himself' (Rookmaaker 1970/1994: 174). For art to move in this direction, of course, would be for it to abandon the sort of seriousness embedded in any ambition to re-enchant the world in the wake of religion. But what else might it do? Wolterstorff is correct, in my view, in his attempt to identify structural analogies between art and religion of the kind that Barzun (as quoted at the end of the previous chapter) denies. But the analogue between aesthetic contemplation and mystical experience is both partial and incomplete. Other, broader structural analogies are required.

What could these be? Traditional religion, Christian or otherwise, provides not merely objects of contemplation, but through them a stimulus and a call to action. The action in question includes what is broadly called 'ethical', and sometimes Christianity has been represented as inspiring and requiring only action of this kind. But this restriction has never proved enduring. Religious action properly so called invariably has two aspects; it is ritualistic and it takes place in a sacred space, that is to say, a place set apart.

Are there analogues to each of these? As far as sacred space is concerned, Wolterstorff finds a clear parallel here too.

To step into the new East Wing of the national Gallery in Washington is to be reminded at once of those great shrines of Christendom, the medieval cathedrals. And to observe the hushed tones and reverential attitudes of those who trudge through those halls is to be put in mind of a procession through the ambulatory of one of those cathedrals. The veneration of bones and sticks and cloths connected with the saints has virtually disappeared from our society. The authenticity of all such objects is suspect to us; and even if it were not, we prefer our religious devotion to be less attached to artifacts. Malraux's suggestion is that this type of veneration has not disappeared from our society without trace. Instead, works of art have replaced relics. (Wolterstorff 1985: 268)

The art gallery as temple. This is to my mind an extremely plausible analogue, and one to be explored at greater length, in a later chapter. Wolterstorff's account of it in this passage, however, draws attention to a seeming disanalogy that is worth investigating further. Relics were displayed and venerated not for themselves in the way that residues of the ancient world are displayed in museums, but because of their historical association with, for example, the lives of saints. The importance of such association also applies to religious art. The religious paintings of the great masters hung (and hang) in churches and cathedrals in virtue not of their form but of their content—namely, biblical stories and episodes from the lives of the saints. Accordingly, their contemplation is not of a purely perceptual kind. Just as the faithful are invited to venerate a fragment of the True Cross because it is the very thing on which the saviour of the world once hung, so the faithful are invited to look through the paintings and sculptures that fill the temple to the people and events they represent.

Of course, it might be said that the Surrealists too want people to look through their works, beyond 'the painted veil', and thereby see in the human condition those elements of the strange and occult that a scientific rationality cannot accommodate. In some of their works, it is hard to see quite how this works. Magritte has a picture expressly entitled *The Human Condition*, in which his astonishing technical mastery enables him to make a painting of sea and sand on an easel continue almost seamlessly the reality of sea and sand beyond. But this suggests that lifting the painted veil makes no difference since there is only the same painted veil beyond, and, if so, by the same token the painter has nothing to reveal.

But this is not the most interesting issue. More important is the question of what the artistic equivalent of historical association might be. It is important for the faithful to dwell on the events the Bible recounts since these comprise the story of their salvation, and the lives of the saints are important objects for Christians to contemplate because they provide patterns of discipleship that can be admired and emulated. It is in this way that religious art moves beyond mere contemplation and provides the sort of inspiration that can be connected with action. What is the artistic counterpart to these?

One answer would be this. The investigation of Nietzsche's (and Arnold's and Malraux's) thought that Art is a natural contender to fill the vacuum left by Religion need not proceed on the assumption that this is a task that each artistic medium must do on its own. If the visual arts cannot provide all the structural analogues with religion, perhaps the other arts can. And at this point in the argument, there is a natural place to turn. If what we require is an analogue to Christian stories, we may find it in the literary arts.

4

Telling a Different Story

RELIGIOUS LITERATURE

In a previous chapter I observed that popular Christianity was alive and well in late nineteenth- and early twentieth-century Europe, long after the intellectual events that are often supposed to have killed it. An important part of the evidence for this contention is the quantity of religious literature in circulation fifty years after Darwin's *Origin of Species* was published. In Britain, but in other places also, much of this literature took the form of tracts and leaflets, expressly directed at both evangelizing and combating specific sins and evils. These tracts were usually distributed free in vast quantities by an army of volunteers and paid 'colporteurs', the cost being met by churches, evangelical societies and wealthy individuals. But there was also a very large amount of religious literature in the narrower sense—that is to say, novels, short stories, and poems—and the popular appeal of this literature was such that it could be sold very profitably. For the purpose of assessing the extent and strength of religious belief within a culture, this second type of literature is more important evidence than the first. A relatively small number of enthusiasts can produce and pay for a very large quantity of printed material, and distribute it to a population that does not take much interest, or even takes no interest at all. But books and stories can only *sell* well if there is widespread demand.

The immense demand for such materials provides powerful evidence of the contemporary religiosity of the United States. A US

Christian fiction catalogue for 2007 lists over 9,000 titles, many of them available in major bookstores. In contemporary Europe such works exist, but are never on display in bookstores. The existence of such fiction is powerful evidence because it reveals a depth of interest in religion that mere statistics about church attendance, weddings, and funerals cannot reveal. All of these can be influenced by social conformity and economic advantage, but no one is obliged to buy and read religious fiction. What is true of the United States now was once true of Europe also (France apart). Until well into the twentieth century 'recreational' religious literature figured prominently in many publishers' lists. One particular instance illustrates a general picture. Peter Drummond, a Scottish seedsman, first published a tract against Sabbath breaking in 1848. From this humble beginning, a huge publishing enterprise developed. Within ten years Drummond had sold eight million copies of its publications across Britain and the empire. By the 1930s the publication of tracts for distribution was more than matched by the publication of all age journals, novels, and books of stories for sale. At its height, the Drummond Catalogue had 2,000 titles, a third of them novels, many with print runs of 50,000 or more (see Brown 2003: 50).

Figures like these, relating to the period to which they do, are important for the debate about secularization. Yet for anyone able to see beyond the confines of a largely secularized culture, the existence and popularity of religious fiction alongside romance and adventure can hardly be surprising in itself. Storytelling has always been a marked feature of the Christian religion, as it has of many others (though not all). The New Testament itself both records stories about Jesus, and recounts stories told *by* Jesus; the Good Samaritan and the Prodigal Son are probably the most famous of these, and have been retold innumerable times, mostly because they have provided the material for 2,000 years of sermons. In this respect, of course, the New Testament is simply continuous with the Old, a large part of the content of which can be classified as 'stories' that, taken together, comprise the distinctive history of Israel. Both Testaments are sacred texts, and the stories they contain are to be accorded a special status. For most of their history, however, Judaism and Christianity have also attributed religious significance to stories that do not fall within the confines of their sacred texts. Obvious instances are Jewish stories of national heroes and notable rabbis, and Christian stories of saints and martyrs subsequent to those of the New Testament. In a religious culture it is inevitable that literary imagination will add to this stock of 'official' stories and generate a distinctive religious fiction. As with other branches of fiction, some of it (most of it, probably) will amount to little more than entertainment, possibly with an 'improving' element. Some of it, though, can be expected to join the ranks of 'great literature'.

These remarks amount to stating the obvious, but the purpose of doing so is to underscore the important fact that telling, retelling, and fashioning new stories are all an important part of the *practice* of religion. In each of the world's major religions, storytelling has a role in the life of the devotee and the adherent, both within and beyond the walls of the temple. In this respect, however, religion seems to be continuous with a more general human practice, because there are few, if any, aspects of life in which storytelling is not to be found.

Why do people tell stories? This is a question without a single answer. Sometimes it is for information, sometimes simply for entertainment. Sometimes, it seems, the storytelling has a much deeper significance, connected in some important way with finding/giving/transmitting meaning to human existence. It is this third reason that is of special interest here. If part (perhaps a large part) of the importance of religious storytelling lies in this connection with meaning, and if it is true that science and rationalism have disenchanted the world by rendering religious belief impossible for the 'modern' mind, and if it is further true that disenchantment is a cause of anxiety because it threatens the meaningfulness of human life, then a crucial task confronting any artistic endeavour to re-enchant the world will be the provision of alternative stories.

HISTORY, PARABLE, AND FICTION

In order to consider the nature of this task more precisely, however, it is essential to observe that religious stories come in importantly different types—'history', 'parable', and 'fiction' chiefly—and it is only the last of these that we could expect art to try to replicate. By 'historical' stories I do not mean those known to be true, or supported by the best available evidence, but stories whose historicity is essential to their authority. Someone who comes to think that the story told in the first fourteen chapters of Exodus never happened, that the Children of Israel were never in, and therefore could never have been delivered from, bondage in Egypt, can go on observing Jewish Passover—but only in the most attenuated sense. History or myth, the Exodus is a good story to tell, since it is full of adventures—the plagues, the crossing of the Red Sea, the drowning of Pharaoh's army, the wilderness wandering, manna from heaven, the delivery of the Ten Commandments, and so on. But if none of this actually happened, then there is and has been no deliverance. The familiar Passover rituals could continue to be regarded with great fondness, and the story told with verve and enthusiasm, but if God did not act on Israel's behalf and set his people free, if the Jews are not His 'Chosen' people, then the Passover rituals cannot amount to a celebration properly so called, because there is nothing to celebrate.

The same point can be made about Christianity, which rests crucially on a salvation history. 'If Christ is not raised,' says St Paul, 'our faith is in vain.' To say that the story of Christ's Crucifixion and Resurrection is essentially historical is to agree with this conditional. At the same time, it is possible to agree with the conditional, while denying the truth of the antecedent. That is to say, someone can hold that the truth of the story of Jesus' death and Resurrection is essential to its having the authority Christians claim for it, while not actually believing it to be true.

In the same sense, the stories of saints and martyrs are importantly historical. It is true that hagiography—the fanciful embellishment of saintly lives and martyrdoms with fantastic events and miraculous actions—is a common feature of such stories, but the exposure of hagiography is destructive of the authority that the life of a saint or a martyr is intended to have. A fabricated life cannot properly inspire, an uneventful death at the end of a quiet life cannot serve as the ultimate act of witness (which is what 'martyr' originally meant), and a saint who never existed cannot be one of the cloud of witnesses that surrounds the Christian and encourages disciples on their way.

Accepting this distinction between stories that are 'historical' and those that are not allows us to remain uncommitted about the historicity of any particular story. To classify the Exodus or the Resurrection as a historical story is only to say that their historical truth or falsehood *matters*, whether we know it or not. There is a fundamental difference between these and other stories, from both the Old and the New Testaments, whose historicity is not so crucial. It had better be the case that Moses existed, but how important is it that there was an actual Job, Ruth, or Daniel? Whichever way we answer this question, the example of the Good Samaritan demonstrates that there are religious stories whose historicity is irrelevant to their importance. Though generally understood as an invented parable, this particular story could as a matter of fact have been a true one. In reply to the lawyer's question 'Who is my neighbour?', Jesus may have been saying 'What do you think about that recent episode on the road to Jericho?'. The philosophical point is that whether or not in this and other parables Jesus had a real case in mind is of no consequence to the significance of the story. If anyone, on discovering that this was not an actual occurrence, were to say 'so it's just a story, then', this would reveal a failure to understand that stories can have a value other than factual accuracy.

Such a failure points up a crucial difference between stories *about* Jesus and stories told *by* Jesus. No one thinks it crucial whether or not the Prodigal Son existed or acted in the way Jesus says he did, or whether he really had a resentful elder brother. This is because it is a *parable*. We might usefully interpret the category of 'parable' broadly to include fables and allegories, both fantastical and mundane. The list of New Testament parables includes that of the sower, which is really an allegory based on an everyday occurrence in the life of the rural peasantry to which it was addressed. But the Bible has much more extravagant allegories also—the story in Daniel of the statue with feet of clay, for example, and the allegory of the four horsemen in the Book of Revelation, both of which have fantastical elements. What makes the parable of the sower an allegory no less than the apocalyptic events narrated in Revelation, is the fact that the elements within it have a one-to-one identity with abstract ideas or concepts. Thus, the sower's seed is 'the word of God', the stony ground on which it falls refers to the hardened hearts who hear it, the weeds that choke the new plants are the cares and occupations of ordinary life that so easily distract, and so on. In a similar fashion, the feet partly of clay and partly of iron are 'a divided kingdom' and the rider of the fourth horse is 'Death'.

In addition to allegories, the category of parable includes fables. These are stories that may have fantastical elements, but do not have the one-to-one correlations that proper allegories do. Among biblical parables we might label the story of Lazarus who lay at the rich man's gate a fable. The most famous stories of this kind, of course, are Aesop's fables, which are not Christian or even religious. But they illustrate the important point that fables, like allegories, can be told for some significant purpose, while being acknowledged as non-historical by those who tell them. 'The Fox and the Grapes' has a point that some will see and others will miss, even though all are aware that foxes cannot talk and do not eat fruit.

It should be evident that drawing this distinction between historical episodes and parables is one way of identifying a number of vexed and important questions regarding Christian belief. Are the miracle stories told of Jesus historical or allegorical/fabulous? To declare them parables rather than history does not necessarily mean that they lose all of their authority. Arguably, the Wedding at Cana and the Transfiguration are stories whose allegorical significance is far more important than their historical accuracy. This is not true of all, however. In the interpretation of New Testament miracles an important distinction is sometimes drawn between 'wonders' and 'signs'. On the former interpretation, miracles are actions that amaze; on the latter, they are actions that reveal. But even if in general we think that the miracles of Jesus are usually to be interpreted as 'signs' rather than 'wonders', it still seems crucial to many of them that they have an ineliminably historical element, that he should actually have *performed* them. The action of restoring sight to the blind may be chiefly a powerful way of conveying a religious message about spiritual blindness, but the action can only speak louder than words if it really took place.

These are not issues to concern us here, however, since the main focus of attention must be a third category—the fictional. By 'fictional' I mean extended literary works of imagination that make no claim to historicity, but are nevertheless realist rather than allegorical or fabulous. Though their characters and locations do not exist, and the events they recount never happened, in some sense they could have. This notion of 'realism' is notoriously difficult to conceptualize satisfactorily, and there are competing accounts of it. Even so, we have an intuitive grasp of the distinction, and can easily give ostensive definitions. Jane Austen's novels are realist, Tolkien's *Lord of the Rings* is not. We might have met an Emma in eighteenth-century England; there is neither time nor place when we might have met a Gandalf.

REALISM AND ROMANTICISM

I shall not attempt here to explicate this concept of realism further, because I want to explore a distinction within the category of the realistic—namely, the distinction between the truthful and the romantic. To a considerable extent these are terms of art that I am deploying for my own purposes, and, since this is something of a departure from their ordinary use, it is essential to explain the idea behind them. Consider the novels of Charles Dickens. These often weave together the truthful and the romantic. *David Copperfield*, for example, is for the most part a story that depicts the realities of struggle, failure, success, friendship, betrayal, and so on. But its final chapter, in which all the storylines are neatly rounded off, with such evident contrivances as Mr Micawber's letter from Australia, abandons truthfulness for romance. 'That would never happen', we can say, but for quite different reasons from those that make us say we would never travel to Middle Earth.

Mere implausibility is not enough, however, to pick out the romantic element, which is captured more precisely, perhaps, by the familiar saying that an ending such as this is 'too good to be true'. In other words, what controls the ending is not understanding, but desire, not how the world is, but how it would be nice for it to be. When Steerforth betrays Copperfield's friendship by seducing Little Emily, Dickens is revealing to us a particular understanding of the moral world in which we live; when he writes the final chapter, he is appealing (pandering some might say) to how we wish the world to be, rather than how we know it to be.

As in this case, the distinction between the truthful and the romantic can be applied within literary works as well as between them. Generally, Dickens combines both. In the preface to *Dombey and Son*, he lays claim to 'the faculty to observe the characters of men'. That Dickens did have this faculty can hardly be disputed. Chapter 31, 'The Wedding', exhibits it brilliantly. But chapter 60, entitled 'Chiefly Matrimonial', shows the other side of Dickens, his willingness to discard observation in favour of making everything come out right in the end. By contrast, George Eliot, another of the great nineteenth-century English novelists, has very little romance in this sense. There are moments of it in *Silas Marner*, but *Middlemarch*, generally regarded as her masterpiece, may be said to exhibit the faculty of observing the characters of men and women throughout.

It would be a mistake to condemn the romantic as simply fanciful distortion. The purpose of romance is not to deceive, but to entertain, and we are under no illusion about (most) happy endings. Anthony Trollope by his own account wrote romances. The plot of a large number of his forty-seven novels is one in which the boy gets the girl (and her fortune) despite all the obstacles society places in the path of true love. Yet in the course of his novels he too reveals himself as having the faculty to observe the characters of men and women, with great acuity. The overall purpose is to entertain, but in the course of accomplishing it he also has things to reveal about human nature and the human condition.

It has long been a matter of philosophical debate as to how works of fiction *as such* can also be concerned with reality—how pure invention could reveal the way things really are. Surely the fictional is to be defined as the imaginary, and hence the polar opposite of the real? Once again this issue is not one to be explored at length here. Since I have defended the view elsewhere (see Graham 2005: ch. 4), I shall simply assert that the crucial point is this. We discover what imaginative literature has to say about life, not by some sort of induction from the real world to the imaginary world of fiction, but by applying the images fiction supplies to the world in which we find ourselves. To understand the importance of this observation it is useful to distinguish between stereotype and archetype. The distinction is owed to Hegel, who contrasts 'characters' with 'formal and abstract representatives of general types'.

[C]haracters should not be merely interests personified . . . abstract presentations of specific passions and aims are always entirely ineffectual; even a purely superficial individualization is wholly unsatisfactory because content and form fall apart as they do in allegorical figures. . . . the chief thing is not a mere wealth of particular traits of character but the all-pervasive individuality which collects everything together into the unity which is itself . . . A mere assembly of different qualities and activities, even if arrayed one by one into a whole, does not provide a living character, for that presupposes a living and richly imaginative creation by the author. (Hegel 1975: 1177–8)

By 'stereotype' (Hegel's 'abstract presentation'), I mean the depiction of a person, an event, or a circumstance that in some way or another generalizes from common experience, and constructs its plots and characters out of the commonplace or generally known. By replacing Hegel's word 'character' with the term 'archetype', my intention is not to change the basic idea, but only to extend it, to include unique imagined localities, contexts, and events as well as persons. In any of these we may find an imaginary entity through which we see and thus come to understand the world in which we find ourselves in new and illuminating ways.

The value of the distinction between stereotype and archetype for present purposes is this. A large part of human storytelling involves romantic stereotypes. There is nothing objectionable in this as such, any more than Hegel's insightful observation that within allegories form and content are wholly separable is an objection to the use of allegory. Stories appeal to a deep-seated human trait, as is evidenced by the ability of very young children to understand and appreciate both narratives and characters. Religious stories, like moral tales, appeal to just this human trait, but they also lay claim to a greater seriousness, and this means that the distinction between the truthful and the romantic must be applied to religious fiction, not just as a classification, but for the purposes of critical assessment. Even if the expression 'religious romance' might sound odd to modern ears, such a thing can exist, and does so when religious fiction trades in stereotypes rather than archetypes. The chief failing is that in a certain sense stereotypes are falsely misleading. Though they seem to depict reality, their romanticism in fact deflects us *from* reality by equivocating between how life is and how we would like it to be.

NARRATIVE, VOCATION, AND MEANING

The issue that concerns us, then, may be stated in this way. Is there an adequate secular equivalent to truthful religious fiction? Implicit in this question is another that needs to be made explicit.

What is the mark or measure of adequacy? To answer this further
question means returning to some of the themes of the opening
chapter, especially those of self-realization and personal vocation.
There is a recurrent and seemingly deep-seated desire on the part
of human beings that their lives should have meaning as well as
value. Consider Marlon Brando's famous and haunting line in the
film *On the Waterfront* when he discovers that he's just been a
pawn in his brother's schemes—'I could have been somebody'. This
cri de cœur captures a hope and a lament that the humblest can
experience. It points us beyond valued experiences, and asks that
both good times and bad 'add up' to something. But what might the
structure of this 'adding up' be? Contrary to the idiom, it seems that
maximized preference satisfaction is not enough. It is not more of
the same, but some quite different structuring that is required. An
obvious alternative structure is narrative, which is to say biography
and autobiography. Normally these are thought of as being reserved
to the great and the good, to those who have specially interesting
or commendable lives, and this implies that a life's adding up to
something requires a crowning achievement of some sort. Yet the
desire to have an autobiographical tale to tell is a desire found among
all sorts and conditions of people. How is the most ordinary person
to 'be somebody'? Since everybody *is* somebody, the question seems
to make no sense, and yet it nonetheless expresses a common and a
deep desire.

In an essay entitled 'Life in Quest of Narrative', Paul Ricœur
brings the distinction between human life and biological life that was
drawn in Chapter 1 above to bear directly on this point. Ricœur's
concern is with the 'way that fiction contributes to making life, in
the biological sense of the word, a human life' (Ricœur 1991: 20),
and this remark provides a helpful way of connecting the theme of
the opening chapter with the topic of this one. How exactly does (or
could) fiction contribute to making a life, and does religious fiction
do it more adequately than any secular equivalent could?

Among contemporary philosophers, it is Alasdair MacIntyre who
has made the concept of narrative central to a philosophical account

of human life. In *After Virtue* he argues at length against the concept of 'self', whose clearest philosophical expression is to be found in existentialism—the self as a free, independent chooser, making choices that are grounded in nothing other than an autonomous will. Though this conception of the self has gained a very wide currency, and underlies a large part of contemporary moral theory and political philosophy, MacIntyre contends that it is deeply incoherent. Part of its incoherence is revealed in the erroneous concept of human action to which it gives rise. For actions to be intelligible it is insufficient for them to be construed as 'behaviour' caused by will or intention. 'There is no such thing as "behaviour" to be identified prior to and independently of intentions, beliefs and settings' (MacIntyre 1981: 194). Actions gain both their identity and their intelligibility by being located within such a context.

We identify a particular action only by invoking two kinds of context, implicitly if not explicitly. We place the agent's intentions, I have suggested, in causal and temporal order with reference to their role in the history of the setting or settings to which they belong. In doing this, in determining what causal efficacy the agent's intentions had in one or more directions, and how his short-term intentions succeeded or failed to be constitutive of long-term intentions, we ourselves write a further part of these histories. Narrative history of a certain kind turns out to be the basic and essential genre for the characterization of human action. (ibid. 194)

Thus far we might suppose that the narrative understanding of action MacIntyre has in mind is essentially retrospective, and indeed MacIntyre lays considerable emphasis on inherited history—the history of the family, clan, country to which we belong, not by choice but by birth. This is a history that cannot be expunged. It is just there, and the point he wants to stress is that, though we can rebel against it, we cannot deny it. A related point is this. Historical stories gain their authority from their historicity, but by the same token they cannot be changed or embellished. In this sense they offer no scope for creatively imaginative engagement. Consequently, like icons and similar paintings, their role in our lives is essentially that of objects of contemplation. In so far as they are understood to recount historical events, the stories of the Exodus, the Incarnation, the Crucifixion, and the Resurrection are there to be contemplated, dwelt on, celebrated. These are acts of appropriation, and it is by means of appropriation that such events come to have a personal meaning, to be part of our story. But for all that, their meaning lies in what they accomplished independently of our own lives and actions—the deliverance of Israel, the salvation of humankind, and so on. In short, whatever their connection with our lives, inherited narratives fit Louis O. Mink's contention that 'stories are not lived but told' (quoted in MacIntyre 1981: 97).

The same point might be made about parables. Although parables usually have practical or moral meaning, a point to make, this meaning lies in analogical application to the hearer, not in practical enactment. A memorable illustration of the difference is to be found in the episode from 2 Samuel where Nathan the prophet tells King David about a rich man who was so mean that he took the lamb of a poor neighbour to feed a guest rather than kill one of his own. On hearing the story, David takes it to be historical and swears to punish the wrongdoer. But 'You are the man!' Nathan tells him, since the story he has just related is in fact a parable directed at David's own conduct in engineering the death of Uriah the Hittite so that he could marry Bathsheba, Uriah's beautiful wife.

Historical stories and parables are narratives that are told. But MacIntyre wants to insist that a narrative structure is built into the intelligibility of living life, and not merely of recounting it afterwards. 'It is because we all live out narratives in our lives and because we understand our own lives in terms of the narratives that we live out that the form of narrative is appropriate for understanding the actions of others' (MacIntyre 1981: 197), and he summarizes his conception as 'the agent as not only an actor, but an author' (ibid. 198).

Ricœur, in a phrase reminiscent of Mink's, identifies a paradox confronting this appeal to fictional storytelling as a source of human meaning: 'stories are recounted, life is lived. An unbridgeable gap seems to separate fiction and life' (Ricœur 1991: 25). Now, if MacIntyre is correct to think of a human being living out a life as, in some sense, the author of that life, then we have the makings of a way in which the gap can be bridged. On Ricœur's analysis, 'anchorage of the narrative in life lies in what could be called the pre-narrative quality of human experience'. That is to say, the life of a human being as a biological entity is a 'story in its nascent state', 'activity and passion in search of a narrative' (ibid. 29) and it is the acquisition of such a narrative that transforms this biological existence into human life. How does such a narrative come to be acquired?

There is an important danger to be avoided here. One conception of acquiring a narrative is where a human being identifies a pre-conceived role to be acted out, something after the fashion of Don Quixote. But this is mistaken on two counts. First, such a conception would make the agent an actor but not an author. Second, it would not in any case serve the purpose, because it could only be *acted out* and never *lived*. A preconceived role makes no allowance for the contingency and open-endedness of human life. We do not know what the future has in store for us, or how long our future will be. So what is required is a non-Quixotic alternative. This is to be found in an ability to forge connections of intelligibility between what happens to us, the decisions we have made in the past, our present choices, and the ways in which they shape or constrain our responses to future events. The key to living a life as opposed to merely existing, therefore, lies in an acquired, and increasingly sophisticated, ability to see and act in accordance with the requirements of narrative intelligibility. We learn to do this in part by imitation, but we are also enabled to forge such connections by the opportunities for understanding that fiction provides.

The idea at work in this suggestion is closely connected to Gadamer's conception of 'the play of art'. Gadamer wants to empha-size the essentially collaborative character of art. That is to say, art objects rely for their existence on a collaboration between artist and audience. In a picture, for instance, 'what is presented to the senses is seen and taken for something' (Gadamer 1967/1986: 29). Dogs and cats, being possessed of vision, can see what is in a picture, but they cannot take it for something (except by chance); only human beings do that, and this 'taking for something' is what makes the picture a picture, rather than just a two-dimensional coloured surface. 'The challenge of the work brings the constructive accomplishment of the intellect into play' and 'the identity of the work is not guaranteed by any classical or formalist criteria, but is secured by the way in which we take the construction of the work upon ourselves as a task' (ibid. 28).

The same point can be made about literary works—'reading is not just scrutinizing or taking one word after another, but means above all performing a constant hermeneutic movement guided by the anticipation of the whole' (ibid. 28). If this is correct, then the reader of fiction is engaged in constructive work, *making* narrative connections, and, if the work is one of seriousness and substance, thereby enabled to make them beyond the confines of the literary, and in life as it is being lived.

It remains to make more precise, however, the connection between narrative intelligibility and meaningful existence. One way of doing so is to deploy as the interconnecting concept an idea discussed briefly in the first chapter—namely, vocation. What is it to be a Christian? We might consider this question from an entirely external point of view, as, say, the compilers of religious statistics do. This will require us to formulate empirical criteria of classification. But such criteria have no practical value; they could not tell anyone how to live *as* a Christian. So, clearly, there is an internal perspective as well, where the issue is not how, for some descriptive or explanatory purpose, Christians are to be identified, but how being a Christian is to be understood by those who want to live a life properly described in this way.

There are two very familiar models of the requisite understanding. The first is what we might call a theological conception: to be a Christian is to hold certain beliefs, to subscribe to certain theological doctrines. The second can be called 'ethical': to be a Christian is a matter of following a distinctive set of rules, to be someone whose conduct of life is determined by a code such as the Ten Commandments or the Sermon on the Mount. These two conceptions can be combined, of course, and usually are. But even in combination they present us with a deeply defective conception of a religious life. To begin with, given the fact that the theological beliefs to which those calling themselves Christians subscribe are often to be defined in opposition to each other (as are the Protestant and Catholic doctrines of the sacraments, for example), it is implausible to suggest that Christian adherence can be characterized as doctrinal unity. And, for reasons that I will not repeat here, it is immensely difficult to identify any shared ethical 'code', especially if we consider Christian ethics over time (see Graham 2001: ch. 1). Second, even if Christian identity could be adequately characterized in terms of some core beliefs and principles, such a characterization would fall on the 'objective' rather than the 'subjective' side of defining a Christian. This is a distinction with which Kierkegaard ends his *Concluding Unscientific Postscript* (Kierkegaard 1992: i. 607–16), and, though there are reservations to be entered about his account of the difference, there is also something essentially correct in it. To characterize being or becoming a Christian in terms of doctrinal subscription, whether theological or ethical, inevitably fails to describe a life of the sort identified by MacIntyre and Ricœur. Such a life comprises *events* in a narrative sequence, whereas the most the theological/ethical conception can conceive of is a series of independent actions governed by theologically informed law. On anyone's reckoning, birth and death are crucial moments in life, as are marriage, the advent of children, the loss of relatives, and so on, and yet none of these is an action falling under a rule. More importantly yet in the present case, a conversion experience like that of Saul on the road to Damascus could not be incorporated into the life of the Christian, since it constitutes neither a belief nor an action. Third, and perhaps most importantly, such a conception does not admit of *personal* life. This is the heart of Kierkegaard's objection, as I understand it. If what is significant is doctrinal subscription and/or action in accordance with a code, then all doctrinal consent and action in accordance with that code is equally significant. The person of the believer and agent falls out of the picture, in just the way that the criminal law is focused exclusively on acts and indifferent to moral motivation and character.

So we need an alternative model. Gadamer (unwittingly, of course) offers us one. To live as a Christian (or a Jew, Muslim, etc.) is to live your life as 'a constant hermeneutic movement guided by the anticipation of the whole'. The 'whole' lies in the ambition of being a Christian (and not merely living like one), and the hermeneutic movement consists in being disposed to forge narrative connections between choices made, actions performed, and events undergone in the light of this whole. In order to succeed in doing this, however, we need to be capable of forging the right kind of connections. We need, for example, to be able to understand past deeds as sins and later ones as acts of repentance, and we need the ability to discern the operation of grace. How are we to learn to do this? One possibility is imitation with the help of a manual. Thomas a Kempis's *De Imitatio Christi* and William Law's *Serious Call to a Devout Life* are famous examples. Still, while it would be difficult to deny that such explicitly devotional works have played an important part in many Christian lives, following a manual of behaviour inevitably falls short of Gadamer's 'constructive accomplishment of the intellect'. What brings this 'into play' is fiction, since fiction requires the reader imaginatively to forge the connections that make the narrative a story. Accordingly, this is where we can locate the role of fiction in the pursuit of a religious vocation. Truthful religious fiction brings faith into play as a 'constructive accomplishment of the intellect', though it is important to stress that this expression should not be given an overly intellectualist interpretation. Such imaginary writings, of which Bunyan's *Pilgrim's Progress* is perhaps an especially plain illustration, offer a very wide range of human beings the possibility that their lives should be made meaningful by the story of their Christian discipleship.

RELIGIOUS FICTION AND ITS ALTERNATIVES

It is important not to confuse the category of 'truthful religious fiction' with truthfully realistic stories about religion. Trollope's Barchester novels have clerical rather than spiritual themes, and, while the characters in them, such as Archdeacon Grantley or Mrs Proudie the Bishop's wife, are characters acutely observed, they are not religious characters in any interesting sense. In this regard, *The Warden* and *Barchester Towers* contrast sharply with, for example, Charlotte Brontë's *Jane Eyre*, written in roughly the same period, which has both religious themes and religious characters. In common with other Victorian novels, *Jane Eyre* has a kind of religiosity that is unattractive to many modern readers, but for all that it is not to be classified as a pious romance. The seriousness of its religious dimension is in part shown by the fact that, in addition to sympathetic portraits of religious characters as diverse as Helen Burns and St John Rivers, Brontë just as readily, and equally powerfully, depicts the corrupted religion of the Revd Mr Brocklehurst, in whom conventional piety is made the mask for partiality and self-aggrandizement. All these characters are archetypes of the religious believer, and understanding the interplay between action, character, and event in each of them involves an engagement of narrative imagination. That is what enables them to contribute to the formation of a life narrative by the reader. There is, of course, no *necessity* of their doing so. Indeed, for most readers nowadays, Brocklehurst is simply a convincing image of a hypocrite. It is only to someone (like Eyre herself) who wants to *be* a Christian that he also represents a *danger*.

This example illustrates a more general point. What makes religious fiction truthful is that, in contrast to pious romance, its archetypes can be examples of corrupted as well as idealized Christians. In order to depict corruption, however, we have to be alive to purity. Someone who thinks that religion itself is bogus cannot depict corrupt forms of it—and cannot really appreciate them either, just as someone who thinks that all motivation is egoistical is incapable of depicting or understanding the phenomenon of 'mixed' motives. James Hogg's *Confessions of a Justified Sinner* and Nathaniel Hawthorne's *The Scarlet Letter* are impressive literary creations and works of spiritual imagination. Their most compelling depictions are of a dark side to Christianity. To describe it (accurately I think) as a 'dark side' is at the same time to deny that it is the whole picture. We might put it this way. Hogg's principal character, the Calvinist Robert Wringham, shows how a sincere conviction of personal salvation can ease the path to damnation. In order to make this statement we need to employ and understand the religious concept of salvation and not just that of damnation.

Even where truthful religious fiction depicts the spiritually admirable, it still differs from the provision of a template. Dostoevsky's Prince Myshkin, though in many ways an archetype of Christian simplicity, is not to be understood as a model for Christians to follow. It is an image in the light of which an autobiographical narrative might be fashioned, not a paragon to be imitated. One of Trollope's few properly religious characters is the eponymous *Vicar of Bullhampton*. Were a contemporary Christian to attempt to emulate his way of life, the result could only be pastiche. Nevertheless, in this character we can find ways in which a natural resistance to 'turning the other cheek' that amounts almost to an innate inability to do so can still find a way of realizing the essence of Christian charity.

It is the mark of truthful Christian fictions, then, that they deal in spiritual and theological matters without romanticism or sentimentality. As in Dickens, both tendencies may be found in a single work, and arguably they are both to be found in *Jane Eyre*. But some paradigmatic examples—religious fictions that completely escape the dangers of romanticism—are to be found in Tolstoy's short stories. The religious purpose of these stories is made evident in the fact that they often begin and end with scriptural quotations, sometimes running to several verses. His *Tales for Children* (1872) and *Popular Stories* (1881/5) were written with the express intention of using his gift as a writer to speak directly to ordinary people about the religious and moral worlds in which they moved. The first of the *Tales for Children* is 'God sees the truth, but waits'. Its title indicates its spiritual purpose, and Tolstoy himself classified it as 'religious art', which meant, in his view, art of the first rank. The story is about Ivan Demetrich Aksënov—imprisoned in Siberia for over twenty years, forever separated from his wife, family, and livelihood, and all for a murder he did not commit. By chance the real murderer arrives in the same prison, and Aksënov is finally vindicated. But Tolstoy eschews any conventional happy ending in which his prosperity is restored and he is reunited with his family. Aksënov dies in prison. The important point is that he does so in a state of grace, brought about by his prayerful struggle with vengeful feeling. The ending to the story is not happiness through the reversal of misfortune, but redemption through its overcoming, which is the properly spiritual ambition.

At the time of their publication, 'What Men Live by' was the most widely circulated of these 'tales', but probably the best known is 'Where Love Is, God Is', the story of a cobbler, Martin Adveich, who dreams that he is to be visited by Christ. The theme of this story, too, is how divine grace is to be encountered in the circumstances of ordinary life, and usually not in the manner expected. Christ does indeed visit Martin, three times in the course of one day, but each time He visits in the form of needy people, not as the supernatural or ethereal apparition the cobbler had expected. Once more, the fiction invites an imaginative construction of the intellect that seeks an understanding of how to lead a Christian life.

There are works of a much larger scale with something of the same nature and purpose. Dostoevsky's great novels—*The Idiot, Crime and Punishment, The Brothers Karamazov*—can all be interpreted as having spiritual themes. So, too, are several of George Eliot's novels, in which religious themes are sympathetically treated, even though Mary Ann Evans herself was a sceptic. *Middlemarch*, her masterpiece, might more accurately be described as having a moral rather than a religious character. To distinguish it in this way is to move the discussion to the issue of alternatives.

What are these alternatives? The major philosophers of the eighteenth and nineteenth centuries gave clearer definition than did preceding centuries to four possible modes of existence—ways in which life might be led. These are the religious, the ethical (or moral), the aesthetic, and the philosophical (on occasions referred to as 'science', or even more generally the 'life of reason'). These divisions of human experience and activity are all to be found articulated and contrasted in Hume, Kant, Hegel, Schopenhauer, Kierkegaard, and Nietzsche. As competing conceptions of ways of life that we might choose, perhaps their most famous account is to be found in the voluminous writings of Kierkegaard. With Hegel chiefly in mind, Kierkegaard dismisses the philosophical as a possible mode of practical life.

For an existing person [he tells us] pure thinking is a chimera when the truth is supposed to be the truth in which to exist. Having to exist with the help of the guidance of pure thinking is like having to travel in Denmark with a small map of Europe on which Denmark is no larger than a steel pin-point. (Kierkegaard 1992: i. 310–11)

This rejection of Hegel's rather grandiose project of delineating and relating the abstractions of Art, Religion, Philosophy, and Morality as modes of spirit is in accordance with the distaste it has generally invoked among philosophers working in what is generally known as the 'analytic' tradition. At the same time, Kierkegaard's exceedingly lengthy existentialist wrestling between ways of life has not much commended itself either, nor, for that matter, Nietzsche's apocalyptic vision of the death of God. And yet the issue to which the consideration of these 'grand' themes has now brought us—the role of fiction in moral life—is one that has received extensive discussion from writers in analytical aesthetics. (For a useful summary and bibliography see Kieran 2006: 356–7.) A major figure in this discussion has been Iris Murdoch, herself both a philosopher and a novelist of some distinction. In her philosophical writings, and especially in *The Sovereignty of Good*, Murdoch tries to fashion an account of morality that will generate something like the religious conception of vocation, but stripped of its theological (though not its metaphysical) underpinnings. And in several of her novels there is the intention (successful or not) to realize something of the same conception in imaginative fictions.

'The morally good life' as the highest form of human existence has a very ancient pedigree of course, and it is easy to place Murdoch (along with several other important contemporary philosophers) within the wider classification of 'virtue ethics'. This label describes a major strand of contemporary moral philosophy that takes a large part of its inspiration from Aristotle and to some extent defines itself in opposition to the dominant alternative between Kantianism and Utilitarianism.

'The moral life' can be construed as a secular conception of vocation, a widespread and attractive alternative to the expressly religious vocation of Jew, Christian, Muslim, and so on. Furthermore, anyone who embraces it can call upon some of the greatest literary works ever written, fiction that 'brings the constructive accomplishment of the intellect into play' as a valuable aid to the pursuit of such a vocation. These would include the classics of Greece and Rome, the works of Shakespeare, Molière, Goethe, and Ibsen, the novels of Fielding, Austen, Stendhal, and Conrad—and even these would constitute only a small part of all the outstanding literature that might be thought of in this way. Nietzsche confronts this alternative with a problem, however. His contention is that the death of God implies the death of 'morality' also, a second death he welcomes with as much enthusiasm as he welcomes the first. As in the case of St Paul's, Nietzsche's conditional—'If God is dead, morality is impossible'—can be accepted without affirming the antecedent.

At the heart of Nietzsche's thesis is a certain conception of 'morality', and the proponents of virtue ethics can claim with considerable plausibility that his strictures apply only to morality construed along generally Kantian or Utilitarian lines. This is in fact the line of thought developed by MacIntyre in *After Virtue*.

The inability of modern moral philosophers to carry through their projects of analysis and justification is closely connected with the fact that the concepts with which they work are a combination of fragmented survivals and implausible modern inventions .... The rejection of the Aristotelian tradition [is] a rejection of a quite distinctive morality in which rules, so predominant in modern conceptions of morality, find their place in a larger scheme in which the virtues have the central place; hence the cogency of the Nietzschean rejection of modern moralities of rules, whether of a utilitarian or of a Kantian kind [does] not necessarily extend to the earlier Aristotelian tradition. (MacIntyre 1981: 239)

This is an important line of thought, but not one to be examined in detail here, since I have already dealt at length with the issues it raises in *Evil and Christian Ethics*. If the argument I advance there is correct, removed from a theistic background, 'morality', even conceived along Aristotelian lines, is not a coherent conception, and of course MacIntyre's development of his project in subsequent volumes also turns for its satisfactory completion to the traditional Christian resources found in Augustine and Aquinas.

Little in philosophy (if anything) can be taken to be settled. In *The Art of Life*, John Kekes makes a sustained and plausible case in defence of 'the morally good life' as a coherent and inspiring 'vocation' for human beings. Kekes discounts religious alternatives as no longer available to the secular mind, but he recognizes another alternative to the moral, namely the aesthetic. It is a contrast made famous (though articulated rather differently) by Kierkegaard in *Either/Or*. This long work closes with a debate between 'the aesthetic' and 'the ethical', which are held to be 'in equilibrium'. If there is a way of transcending that equilibrium, it lies in 'the edifying thought that against God we are always in the wrong'. For anyone to whom this 'edifying thought' is impossible, the equilibrium must be transcended some other way. If we assume (*contra* Kekes) that 'the morally good life' is fatally undermined by its separation from religion, the burden of providing us with an alternative 'edifying thought' must lie with the aesthetic, which is, of course, the topic of this book. At this juncture, however, the issue can be given a more precise formulation. Can we identify a truthful fiction that would enable us to forge the narrative connections necessary for an aesthetic 'vocation', a life of art?

FINDING AN AESTHETIC ALTERNATIVE

There is one very obvious candidate—James Joyce's semi-autobiographical work *Portrait of the Artist as a Young Man*. This recounts a Catholic upbringing in late Victorian Ireland, and its rejection. Like any great work, it is a novel full of subtleties and complexities, and arguably only a forerunner to a work of even greater complexity—Joyce's huge masterpiece *Ulysses*, probably the greatest work in twentieth-century English literature. There is a danger, accordingly, that pressing it into service as the illustration of a philosophical thesis will result in distortion. Nevertheless, the degree to which it articulates, and is itself a manifestation of, the ambition that the autonomy of the aesthetic be the liberating successor to religion is striking.

The hero of *Portrait* is Stephen Dedalus, and the story of his gradual rejection of Catholicism constitutes the novel. This rejection is the explicit topic of a long conversation between Stephen and his fellow student Cranley, in which Stephen confirms his loss of faith and Cranley tests its depth and rationale. The rejection, it emerges, is neither mere rebellion nor rooted in intellectual obstacles to belief. 'It is a curious thing', says Cranley, 'how your mind is supersaturated with the religion in which you say you disbelieve' (Joyce 2003*a*: 261). Such supersaturation we may suppose to be Joyce's as well, and it is precisely this that gives the novel its power and importance, because it enables Joyce, and hence the reader, to feel the pull of the vision that has to be replaced by depicting its depth and strength. Indeed, Stephen declares that the Catholicism he can no longer accept forms a 'logical and coherent' system, and concedes that its central doctrines may even be true. What motivates his rejection is something different from the fear of falsehood. 'I fear', he says 'the chemical reaction which would be set up in my soul by a false homage to a symbol behind which are amassed twenty centuries of authority and veneration' (ibid. 265). The hope, in other words, is not theological truth, but spiritual freedom. This divorce between the theological and the spiritual is crucial. Dedalus's hope is 'to discover the mode of life or of art whereby [the] spirit could express itself in unfettered freedom' (ibid. 267). The aim of the novel is to disclose this new mode in the story of his recourse to art.

At the end of the novel, Dedalus breaks into the first person, and, as he leaves home, declares: 'I go to encounter for the millionth time the reality of experience and to forge in the smithy of my soul the uncreated conscience of my race' (ibid. 275–6). Expressed in the first person, this ambition has an element of the absurd. How could one person forge the conscience of a race? But that is why it is important to recall the novel's title—Portrait of an *Artist*. It is artistic imagination that is to constitute the smithy out of which a new vision of human life will emerge, and that vision will be of life as itself an aesthetic expression. The ambition is strikingly in tune with that of (some) American Abstract Expressionists who out of 'self-examination, self-reassurance and self-expression' aimed to create 'accessible symbols and metaphors for "modern man"' (Hess and Grosenick 2005: 10).

Ulysses is the culmination of Joyce's vision, but even by the time *Portrait* was published it was already a vision in the making. His collection of stories—*Dubliners*—contains several preliminary sketches for *Ulysses*. The fifteen stories are mostly time-slice portraits of people and events rather than extended narratives. They can plausibly be regarded as literary objects of contemplation, and their purpose is 'epiphanic', the creation of moments of revelation and seeing. What is seen, however, is not the weird, the unconscious, or the occult, as in Surrealist paintings, but the ordinary, the everyday. And yet these sketches in words are in many ways the literary equivalent of the Surrealists' paintings. In the midst of the ordinary, something arresting is disclosed, something to stir into existence a new consciousness. *Ulysses*, on a much vaster scale, can be understood in the same way. Though nearly 1,000 pages long, it is the depiction of a single day, and the events that unfold within it, while in the broadest sense a narrative, amount to nothing like a plot.

Could the emergent vision be the newly created conscience of the race, as Dedalus in *Portrait* hopes? One difficulty in the way of its being so is this. Even were it possible to construct secular versions of sin, conversion, and redemption, these stories are epiphanic rather than parabolic. They are literary objects of contemplation that give us pause for thought. Unlike the Tolstoy *Tales*, and popular religious literature more generally, the compelling episodes in *Dubliners* are not really stories at all. They do not require us to forge narrative connections, and they present no biographical structure through which we might ourselves seek meaning. This is especially evident in the story 'Grace'. Its title suggests a quasi-religious theme, a suggestion confirmed to some degree by the episode it recounts. Tom Kernan, a small-time, failing businessman, has drunk too much. He falls down the pub stairs and bites a piece out of his tongue. His friends determine to make this a turning point. His long-suffering wife, for whom religion 'was a habit . . . suspected that a man of her husband's age would not change greatly before death' but raised no objection to their manipulating him into attending a Catholic retreat for businessmen. They assemble in the Jesuit church, Gardiner Street, and Father Purdon begins to preach. But there the episode ends. No account is given of the effect of the retreat or of anyone's future conduct. We are not invited to make anything of it, only to contemplate.

The problem, as with Surrealism, is self-consciousness. In *Portrait*, Joyce is self-consciously an artist. This is a necessary feature of art's autonomy from craft and patronage, the 'twenty centuries of authority and veneration' from which the aesthetic spirit must be liberated in order to 'express itself in unfettered freedom'. At the same time, along with Magritte and in common with the art of modernism in general, such self-consciousness brings with it a kind of implosion or internal destruction. Ulysses invites comparison with Greek mythology, and originally Joyce gave Homeric titles to all the chapters. This is just one aspect of the novel's intense self-consciousness both as a literary construct and as one standing in a long tradition that must itself come to self-consciousness. Declan

Kiberd, in his introduction to the Penguin Classics edition, quotes the German critic Friedrich Schlegel writing in 1800. Any newly forged mythology, says Schlegel, 'must be the most artificial of all works of art, for it is to encompass all others'. This, Kiberd remarks, was 'an astonishingly accurate prediction of the self-critical recuperation of Homeric mythology in Ulysses', which foretells 'the self-destructive way in which Joyce, by making an inventory of previous literary styles, appeared to exhaust the possibilities of literature in the book to end all books' (Joyce 2000: p. xxi).

Of course, to infer from a brief examination of Joyce that any attempt on the part of modern literature to forge a new mythology must fail would be to generalize wildly from a particular instance. In fact, it is possible to find the same phenomenon elsewhere, both in Irish literature and beyond. As noted before, W. B. Yeats, deprived of Christian mythology by Darwinian biology, famously returned to Ireland's ancient myths in an attempt to forge a new mythology of his own. Similarly, the Scottish novelists Neil Gunn and Lewis Grassic Gibbon, working their way out of the shadow not of Catholicism but of Calvinism, struggle to convey a new spirituality rooted in the land and expressed in a kind of acceptance of the 'given' reminiscent of Engels's concept of 'freedom as the recognition of necessity' (which Engels attributes to Hegel).

All these literary authors, I think it can be argued, encapsulate an important inner dynamic that is at work beyond the confines of literature, and is to be found in all manifestations of 'modern' art. It is a dynamic that arises almost inevitably from the ambition to secure art's autonomy. The simplest and commonest way of expressing the ambition of an art that is more than craft and yet freed from the subservience of patronage is in the slogan 'art for art's sake'. The trouble is that this same slogan sits ill with the slogan that might be said to be Tolstoy's—'art for life's sake'. Yet, if art is to re-enchant a post-religious world, it is precisely a replacement for Tolstoy's 'religious' art that must be sought. How is this to be done? All modernist movements have asserted their independence by reacting against the inherited and the conventional. It is an attitude that creative artists have tended to revel in. But ironically, in their castigation of the world, far from achieving a 'transfiguration of the commonplace', artists have simply established a greater gulf between their activities and those of ordinary life. Dedalus, like Joyce, leaves Ireland and the ordinary Catholic life it represents for Art. This is symptomatic. Art in the modern period has won its autonomy by its distance from everyday life. But, as Barzun observes:

> To be valid, the idea of redemption by art would have to be just the opposite—popular and democratic. Secular salvation, like religious, must be open to all who seek it, as Tolstoy insisted. But we all know that high art is difficult . . . It is only in old fashioned sentimental novels that the hero betrayed in love decides to live thanks to his violin. Real artists are not redeemed and continue to curse the world. They feel the flames of Hell and not the felicities of Heaven. (Barzun 1974: 89)

Though Arthur Danto has made famous the idea that modern art is the 'transfiguration of the commonplace', the contrary is more plausible—that modern art is, for the most part, an 'alienation of the commonplace'. So far, of course, we have explored only the arts of painting and literature. Whether things might be different elsewhere is the question that will orient the further exploration of music, architecture, and festival.

5

Singing a New Song

ART MUSIC

Art's aspiration to re-enchant a world disenchanted by the demise of religion derives much of its plausibility from the fact that the history of the arts in Western culture is one closely tied up with that of Christianity. Nowhere is this more evident than in the case of music. Music, obviously, pre-dates Christianity, and as far back as we can discover there seems to have been something akin to ceremonial music, even if in many cases we don't know how it sounded. But the development of tonal or 'Western' music is inextricably conjoined with its use for Christian worship. Of course, there is now a vast amount of composed music that has no connection with religion, and almost certainly this makes up the large majority of all music in existence. Nevertheless, the main impetus to music's development into the spectacular cultural accomplishment that it has become was its religious function. Psalm 150 (which dates from roughly 550 BC) extols the use of voice and instrument in worship, so we may suppose music to have been part of ancient Judaism, and unaccompanied singing was part of the Christian liturgy since the earliest days of the Church. It seems, however, that the use of music in the Jewish and Christian religions was discontinuous. The Psalms appear not to have been sung in synagogues for centuries after the destruction of the Second Temple in AD 70, and the earliest Christian hymns did not have Psalms for texts. The New Testament mentions singing hymns at the Last Supper (Matt. 26: 30), and musical elements that would later be used in the Roman Rite can be found in the third century BC. The practice of singing Psalms as part of the daily round of prayer began with the desert monks who followed St Anthony. In the late fourth century AD, St Ambrose introduced antiphonal singing to the Western church, and by the sixth century this had produced Gregorian chant, the foundation of 'classical' music as we now know it.

One important consequence of this history is that the liturgical requirements and theological themes of Christianity lie at the heart of the greatest musical works of all time—Byrd's *Mass for Four Voices*, Monteverdi's *Vespers* of 1610, Bach's *St Matthew Passion*, Handel's *Messiah*, Beethoven's *Missa Solemnis*, Verdi's *Requiem*. This greatly attenuated list is impressive, but the connection between religious practice and the development of music goes much deeper. It includes the emergence of the scales in which the vast majority of music has been composed since *c*.1600, the instruments by which it was played (notably the pipe organ), and the forms in which it was composed (polyphony and harmony).

As with literature, long past the point when evolutionary biology and Higher Criticism are generally supposed to have dealt Christianity fatal blows, we can find music being composed, played, and sung for religious purposes. Many of the greatest nineteenth-century composers were still composing masses, anthems, and cantatas late in the century—Bruckner, Tchaikovsky, Verdi, for example—as were several well-known twentieth-century composers—Rachmaninov, Fauré, and Britten are cases in point. In fact, some of the most influential composers of the second half of the twentieth century—Olivier Messiaen, Henryk Górecki, Arvo Pärt, John Tavener, and Karl Jenkins are notable instances—are thought of chiefly as composers of religious music, although their music is of many kinds. Even composers generally identified with the modernist avant-garde—Francis Poulenc and György Ligeti, for instance—have composed religious works. The Christian religion thus continues to be a major presence in modern musical composition.

At the same time, as is the case with the other arts, in the course of its development music has also sought autonomy, to pursue its own aims freed from subservience to liturgical and other ceremonial functions. The most evident manifestation of this, and the thing that made it possible, was the music of the concert hall—what is sometimes called 'art' music (the term I shall employ). The development of art music is relatively recent, and relatively rapid. It coincides with the spread of purpose-built concert halls across late eighteenth- and early nineteenth-century Europe, though these are more effect than cause. It takes some mental effort nowadays to remember that sitting down and deliberately listening to music for its own sake is not something that human beings have done for very long. The practice came about as the result of a sort of dialectical process between ever-more sophisticated composition, new cultural practices made possible in part by rising prosperity, and a resulting change in the social status of musicians. Musical genius was not itself enough. Even Mozart could not command the undivided attention of those who had paid him to compose and play. 'Madame and her gentlemen never interrupted their drawing for a moment . . . so I had to play to chairs, tables and walls,' he wrote to his father about a salon concert for the Duchesse de Chabot (quoted in Shiner 2001: 130). The practice of listening to music for its own sake had to be established. Once it had been, the commercial possibilities of this practice stimulated increased social provision for their exploitation. In turn, commercialization became a huge stimulus to composition. Thus the purpose-built concert hall where specially commissioned pieces were played came into existence, and, with it, the social practice of concert-going was added to the activity of music-making.

Something similar may be said of the development of the theatre. At one time, audiences sat on the stage talking, eating, and drinking during even the best efforts of actors and playwrights. The idea of giving exclusive attention to the drama, and the requisite practice of sitting quietly in the audience, had to come about. So, too, with the development of the art gallery. Visitors to the Louvre, a former palace that the French revolutionaries turned into an early version of the art museum as we now know it, had to be taught how to behave, and signs were posted telling them not to sing and play games in its long corridors. Art, like Religion, needs its institutions, and it has found them in the theatre, the art museum, and the concert hall, all of them cultural phenomena whose significance is a subject to be returned to. For the moment, however, our exclusive concern is with music.

The emergence of art music is a vital step in music's quest for autonomy, but art music is itself the outcome of three other important developments. The first of these is the evolution of composition as a musical activity distinct from performance. In improvisation the two are identical and inseparable; the composer and the performer are one and the same. What their separation permits is multiple and repeated performance of 'the same piece'. It thus allows the identification of nameable pieces of music. Indispensable to the separation of composition from performance is the ability to write music down. As the musicologist Karol Berger has observed: 'The importance of writing resides in the fact that the written text makes it possible for music to become an object available for scrutiny independently of the real time of a performance' (Berger 2002: 117). This means that music can become subject to closer attention and analysis, and styles of composition can be imitated, amended, and developed. Even more importantly, it provides a powerful stimulus to originality. A third crucial factor is the development of 'abstract' music—that is, music without words, practical function, or conventional association. The process of abstraction gives music a distinct artistic medium in which it works—namely, pure sound or sonic material. Composition thus becomes comparable to painting, whose distinctive medium is the visual.

These developments all combined to create a conception of art music in which nameable composers working with distinctive materials create nameable works that become objects for the exclusive aesthetic attention of audiences. They thus put music on a par with painting and poetry, the other 'fine arts' as the eighteenth century understood this term. It is in this way that music rose above its secondary status to become a sphere for autonomous creative genius. At the end of this trajectory came compositions such as Beethoven's symphonies and late quartets, sonic artworks that have probably never been rivalled and may never be. The development of art music had a number of very important consequences. Chief of these is that it gradually came to assume (or to be given) the role of paradigm for all music. Of course, no one could fail to note that a vast quantity of music continued to be played and heard (and composed) outside the concert hall—folk music, dance music, ceremonial music, and church music, to name its principal varieties. What is commonly called 'classical' music was always only one among many of music's manifestations. But, implicitly and explicitly, it was art music that came to be considered 'music proper', which is to say, music in its purest and finest form. This made it definitive of the form to which other forms aspire, and thus the form in comparison with which they are to be regarded as inferior. It was this comparison that generated, and still sustains, the secondary, or even second-class, status frequently accorded to other types of music, jazz and folk as well as rock and pop. A further major consequence was that music as an art came to be identified with composers and their works rather than performers and performances. It was great composers, not great singers or players, who took their place in the artistic pantheon alongside the great painters and sculptors, their compositions being treated in much the same way as great paintings and statues. This equivalence then reinforced and was sustained by a theoretical development in the eighteenth century—namely, the emergence of 'aesthetics' as a branch of philosophy. The term, as is well known, was coined by Alexander Baumgarten, but the idea was given its most sophisticated and influential philosophical articulation by Kant. Having explored the foundations of knowledge and morality, Kant then perceived the need of a third *Critique*, because he identified in 'the aesthetic' a special form of attention or 'judgement', which was neither theoretical nor practical, but consisted in the disinterested contemplation of the beautiful for its own sake. By this account, the value of artistic genius is derivative, a consequence of the ability to create beautiful works for aesthetic contemplation.

Art music appears to fit this bill perfectly. If art music is construed as a kind of 'painting in sound', its purpose and value is to provide us with sonic objects equivalent to the visual objects of the great masters. This has a further important consequence. If the value of music lies in the disinterested contemplation of the beautiful, listening, rather than singing or playing, comes to be regarded as the primary mode of engagement, and composition rather than performance the principal creative activity.

Once art music is taken to be the paradigm of music proper, it is easy to see how its autonomy from religion is to be understood. It is importantly *sui generis* in three respects. First, it involves acts of pure creativity whose productions are primarily objects of contemplation. Second, these are to be listened to for their own sake. Third, this activity of contemplative listening takes place in buildings specially set aside for that purpose. To construe art music as (almost literally) the apotheosis of music, or music in its highest form, faces three corresponding difficulties, however. First, it ignores, or at any rate discounts, the fact that musical engagement is not confined to contemplative listening. While it may be true that to some extent a piece of music is the sonic analogue of a picture, unlike painting (icons apart) music is a *performing* art. What is more, the performer is also an artist, and not simply a means of realization in the way that the paintbrush and canvas are. Second, given the history of art music over the course of the twentieth century, if art music is the paradigm, then culturally music has been marginalized almost as much as established religion, possibly more so. According to Berger, 'no other group of artists now active have lost as much of their former public as have twentieth-century composers of art music' (Berger 2002: 110). Third, the conception of music as 'painting in sound' leaves it unclear precisely what the value of music could be. Each of these difficulties is worth examining at greater length.

DIONYSUS VERSUS APOLLO

One of the very few philosophers to question the philosophical presuppositions of art music was Nietzsche. In *The Birth of Tragedy* he rejects the idea that music is an art in the same way that painting and sculpture are.

Music obeys quite different aesthetic principles from the visual arts, and cannot be measured according to the category of beauty . . . [a] false aesthetic . . . has grown used to demanding, on the basis of a concept of beauty that prevails in the world of the visual arts, that music should provide an effect similar to that of works in the visual arts—the arousal of pleasure in beautiful forms. (Nietzsche 1886/1993: 76–7)

In articulating the distinctiveness of music, he draws what is now a well-known distinction between 'the Apollonian' and 'the Dionysian'.

Unlike all those who seek to infer the arts from a single principle, the necessary spring of life for every work of art, I shall fix my gaze on those two artistic deities of the Greeks, Apollo and Dionysus. For me they are the vivid and concrete representations of two worlds of art, utterly different in their deepest essence and their highest aims. (ibid. 76)

'Between the Apolline plastic arts and Dionysiac music', he says, there is a 'tremendous opposition', a 'yawning abyss'. The visual and plastic arts manufacture images whose purpose is to catch our attention and invite our contemplation. This contemplation, however, is passive. Other than the direction of attention itself, it involves no practical activity on our part. By contrast, to be moved by the spirit of Dionysus is to go beyond mere contemplation, because Dionysus is a spirit that takes possession of us and impels us into action. The difference is most easily illustrated in dance music. Dance music is not just something to listen to contemplatively. In fact, it takes a special effort to do so, since there is a quality in the music that impels us into activity, that sets our feet tapping.

Something is missing from our engagement with dance music if we merely sit quietly listening and never take to the floor. This is not just a feature of dance music. Precisely the same point can be made about other kinds of music as well. Folk songs, national anthems, rousing choruses tempt us to sing along. And we are right to yield to the temptation, because singing, not listening, is the proper form of engagement with this kind of music.

Nietzsche is correct in wanting to emphasize a distinctive spirit at work in music, but it is clear nonetheless that some music can be regarded in a largely Apollonian light—namely, art music. To take this as the paradigm for *all* music, however, leads to a distorted understanding even within the world of art music itself. For example, it is not uncommon for singing groups to stage concerts of Elizabethan madrigals. It is easy to see why. There is a large stock of this beautiful music, cleverly written on themes that range from the touching to the humorous. Nevertheless, for an audience, a whole programme of madrigals soon begins to pall. This is because madrigals are written to be sung, not listened to. Consequently the form of engagement proper to them is one of active performance not passive listening. The best way to appreciate their beauty and ingenuity is to sing them. Though they are clearly products of the same development that gave us the music of the concert hall, merely listening to them is a poor substitute. In a similar fashion, concert programmes composed entirely of Strauss waltzes and polkas, John Philip Sousa marches, or Scottish reels and strathspeys very quickly become boring. All these forms of music require a Dionysian rather than an Apollonian form of engagement. But the important point, the one that Nietzsche's slightly exotic references to ancient gods gives us a way of stating, is that singing, dancing, and marching are forms of engagement *with the music*. They are not separable activities that the music merely serves to accompany. It is this truth, and the possibilities it alerts us to, that is in danger of being lost when the music of the concert hall is treated as the paradigm of all music.

The Apollonian/Dionysian contrast is not confined to the difference between the music of the concert hall and the music of the ballroom. Dionysian engagement is a possibility with respect to *all* kinds of music because of music's essential character as a performing art. Thus, while one way of engaging with (say) Beethoven's *Moonlight Sonata* is certainly by listening to it, another is by playing it. Often we tend to think of playing as nothing more than the means by which music can be heard, a tendency powerfully reinforced by the invention of recording technology. But the error in this way of thinking is that it makes too great a concession to the philosophical presuppositions of art music. Practical engagement with the very greatest musical compositions can be open to amateur players and singers, and this engagement is in no way diminished by the fact that the sound they produce may fall far short of anything that would qualify for concert performance. Even when my skills as a pianist are limited, I can engage directly with some of the greatest works ever composed. To appreciate this possibility, though, we have to abandon the conception of music as 'painting in sound'. It is not just dancing and marching but music itself that impels and makes possible a distinctive form of activity. This has no parallel in painting. If, as an amateur painter, I attempt to paint the Mona Lisa, this is not a different form of aesthetic engagement with the works of Leonardo, but just a form of copying. Something similar can be said about poetry, public recitations notwithstanding. If I try to write poetry in the style of John Donne, the most this can accomplish is pastiche. Great paintings and great poems are Apollonian by nature; they admit only of contemplative reception.

In *The Birth of Tragedy* Nietzsche's primary concern is with ancient Greek tragedy. The plays of Aeschylus and Sophocles were written for and performed at religious festivals in Athens. While the main parts were taken by individual actors wearing masks, a Chorus comprised of ordinary citizens also had an important role in the plays, often chanting its lines in a musical style. Nietzsche (whose father was a Lutheran pastor) finds a modern counterpart to this in the Bach Passions. These dramatic depictions of the arrest, trial, and Crucifixion of Christ were written, not for concert performance (which is how we most often hear them today), but for the liturgical observation of Good Friday in the Lutheran church. In addition to orchestra, soloists, and a choir of trained singers, they include 'chorales', which is to say traditional hymns harmonized by Bach. There is uncertainty among musicologists as to whether these chorales were in fact sung by everybody present. A number of considerations make it unlikely, but the issue is not an especially crucial one. The more important point is that the chorales were identifiable to the worshippers as 'their' hymns, and by means of this identification a unity was created between the congregation, the Evangelist's narrative, the drama of the choruses, and the sublime art of the arias.

Whether or not the congregation sang on Good Friday, Bach's chorales are hymns, a version of those that Luther had expressly introduced 200 years earlier in place of the complex polyphonic music of the pre-Reformation Church. He did so as a way of extending to ordinary people a more enriching engagement with music in worship. Being a passionate enthusiast for musical excellence, though, the distinguishing mark of Luther's hymns was not naivety, but familiarity. The harmonizations to which they were set by Lutheran musicians made them compositions of a very high order. When transformed by Bach into his organ preludes, also for use in church, they exhibit a musical genius that has rarely been matched. Many of these preludes require a high degree of skill on the organ, though some are relatively simple; the chorales can be sung by almost anyone. Left in their liturgical context, therefore, they constitute an occasion when ordinary people can be practically engaged with the musical genius of a great composer.

Of course, both the chorales and the preludes can be converted into art music for concert performance, as they frequently are. When this happens, for all but the performers the music is indeed a kind of 'painting in sound' that the audience is invited to contemplate, which is just how the Kantian aesthetic construes it. It is a construal we have reason to reject on at least two counts. First, by attributing value to music-making only in its role as a necessary condition for the realization of sound objects, the Kantian aesthetic confines the activities of playing and singing to the role of means rather than understanding them to be ends in themselves. It thereby discounts nearly all music-making, because little or no value is to be attributed to the (relatively) mediocre playing or singing of great music. If performance is valuable only as a means by which the intentional sound object imagined by the composer is realized for the purposes of listening, then poor attempts at such realization can have value only in so far as they are necessary preparatory steps. With the invention of sound recording, the player who is never going to reach a standard better than average can give up without loss. The implication is that for most people experience of music must become further and further removed from musical activity. Actual performance by music lovers, on their own or in groups, ceases to have value because even cheap recordings realize the art object better than amateurs could ever do themselves, and recordings of the very best performances are widely available. Ironically, despite being taken as paradigmatic, art music thus generates a reason for people to stay away from the concert hall. With the arrival of acousmatic or electro-acoustic music, this process is complete, since 'music' ceases altogether to be a performing art (or as I should prefer to say, music is subsumed within a much wider category of 'sonic art'; see further Graham 2007).

Second, the displacement of music-*making* by music-*listening* breaks the connection between creation and inspiration. In Chapter 1, I explicated the concept of inspiration in terms of motivation to act. Now music-making is itself activity, and so anyone who sits down and attempts to play a piano composition, or joins others for the purposes of singing choral works, is inspired to act. The creative imagination of the composer motivates them directly. But, once music is construed as a sonic equivalent of painting, the question that arises for Surrealism and the visual arts generally arises for music also. How does creativity inspire those who merely contemplate its products? What is it that they are inspired to do? As we shall see in due course, these questions represent important problems for art's ambition to re-enchant the world in the wake of religion.

FUNCTIONALITY, AUTONOMY, AND CONTINUITY

Before addressing these questions directly, however, there is another issue to explore, and it is one brought to the fore by the case of J. S. Bach. Described by Wagner as 'the most stupendous miracle in all music', Bach ranks among the greatest masters of the music out of which art music comes. However, his own conception of music was not that of an autonomous art, but of something deeply subservient to religion: 'To the greater glory of God and that my neighbour may be benefited thereby' is one of his dedications. Commonly called 'God's craftsman', he accepted that his task was to write for contemporary use and practical purposes. This partly explains both Bach's vast output, and why a large quantity of it went unpublished in his lifetime. While he did compose a great deal of purely instrumental music, his vocal and choral compositions, and most of his organ pieces, were written for liturgical purposes. In short, Bach was a practical rather than an art musician. Furthermore, though it has sometimes been suggested that his music owed relatively little to his religious beliefs, more recent discoveries (see Leaver 2004) have confirmed the opinion of one commentator that 'his North German Protestantism was at the root of all his art' (Kennedy 1996).

These facts raise important questions. First, how does the music of this supreme master stand in relation to the autonomous art music of the concert hall? The problem arises in so far as we think that the artistic integrity of music requires it to escape extrinsic functionality. Karol Berger is an advocate of this view, and he expresses it very clearly.

The contrast between autonomous and functional music is between music made and heard for its own sake and music that is nothing but a means of some other practice. (Berger 2002: 116)

Its artistic character is the basis for music's claim to autonomy, which implies that, while art music is autonomous, popular music is functional. . . . the separation of composition from performance and the survival of the products

of composition as written texts independent of performances are the two
defining features of art, as opposed, to popular, music. (ibid. 118)

The clear implication of this seems to be that most of Bach's music
is 'nothing but a means of some other practice'—in this case, the
religious practice of the Lutheran church. Understandably, given
Bach's status, Berger does not want to draw this inference, and
he thinks he can avoid it by appealing to the 'internal aims' of
music.

It is precisely the continuity of music's internal aims, as opposed to its
external functions, that made possible the retrospective inclusion of works
of Bach, Monteverdi, and Josquin in the canon of great art music even
though the external functions of their music changed. (ibid. 116)

Not everyone is so confident that retrospective inclusion of this
kind is possible. The British philosopher Michael Tanner writes:

We are no longer living in a Christian society, in any serious sense, and most
of us are not Christians. . . . And yet we depend for much of our emotional
and spiritual succour on art and teaching that not only presupposes the
truth of Christianity, but actively propagates it. Many an atheist thinks that
[Bach's] *B Minor Mass* is one of the greatest works of art: that is what I feel.
But I am not at all clear that I should. (Tanner 1976–7: 145)

When Bach's *St Matthew Passion* or Monteverdi's *Vespers* are
removed from their liturgical context, the external function for
which they were written is abandoned. If they are not to become
entirely meaningless or worthless, like the observances of ancient
Greek religion (sacrificing a cock to Asclepius, say), then they must
secure some other end or purpose. Berger's concern is with music's
autonomy. He draws on Alasdair MacIntyre for his concept of a
practice, and identifies two essential features. 'First, a practice is
characterized through the "goods" it realizes. Second, the relative
success, or lack thereof is measured by the practice's "standards of
excellence" ' (Berger 2002: 111). A little later he adds: 'A practice is
autonomous because it has aims of its own, and does not derive them
from another practice' (ibid. 115). In the light of this definition he

wants to say that art music is an autonomous practice because it has its own 'goods' and standards of excellence. The retrospective inclusion of Bach in the canon means that, though Bach himself meant to realize the 'goods' of a religious practice, he also, somewhat inadvertently, realized some of the 'goods' that matter to art music. And, whatever Bach's own intention, by art music's standards the goods he realized are to be judged excellent.

This raises one obvious question: why should we judge Bach by the standards of art music, rather than the standards of Christian devotion by which he himself expected to be judged? In a way, this is a less important question than a different, though related one. Suppose someone were to say: removed from its religious context, Bach's music has lost its value. How is the protagonist of art music to reply? Somehow we have to ensure that the 'goods' internal to a practice connect with values beyond that practice, otherwise 'autonomy' is reduced to isolation. In illustration of this point consider the case of cricket, which Berger uses as an example. There are goals internal to cricket—scoring runs, and bowling out the opposing team, for instance—and there are internal standards by which it is judged whether these have been done excellently or not; successful strokes of the bat can be beautifully controlled or just lucky. But if we sever all connection between these internal goals and things regarded as values off the cricket pitch—dexterity, graceful movement, strategic thinking, the deployment of tactics, pleasure, excitement, and so on—the result is a practice that is entirely inward looking, and whose goals and values are confined to people who quite fortuitously happen to share them. To treat the scoring of runs in and of itself as a worthwhile goal is idiosyncratic, and to be equated with eccentric hobbies such as the obsessive collecting of intrinsically worthless objects.

So too with music. The autonomy essential to it as a practice risks severing any connection with wider human interests, and to articulate this autonomy in terms of internal goods is to risk confining its attraction to those who just happen to find these things attractive. Arguably, this is exactly why the audiences for classical music have become so very small in comparison with the audiences for other sorts of music. Berger is aware of this situation and has an illuminating analysis of its cause, though it is not one that it would be strictly relevant to consider here. Our concern is with the broader philosophical task of finding a conceptual middle ground. On the one hand, we have to explain how a practice can be truly autonomous and yet avoid what we might call vicious internality. On the other, we have to establish a connection with values external to the practice while maintaining its autonomy.

In the case of music, an appeal is commonly made to pleasure or entertainment as a way of forging this connection. Human beings value pleasure, and music is one way in which they obtain it. This response encounters several difficulties, however. Most obviously, since it is undeniable that people derive pleasure from rock and pop, folk and jazz, this cannot be the way to isolate the value of art music in particular. Moreover, just because different people get pleasure from different kinds of music, locating the value of art music in terms of the pleasure it gives generates no ground upon which it can be commended to people with different musical tastes. But, in any case, pleasure seems too mundane a value to do the work that the enthusiasts for art music require. Partly this is because it does not give us reason to rank it higher than other, more humble recreational activities such as gambling, games, or pantomime, which are also pleasurable. But neither can the appeal to pleasure sustain any discrimination between the supreme genius of Beethoven or Mozart, and the more modest talents of a minor composer like Hamish MacCunn. The pleasure obtained from listening to music, we might say, is too contingent; it cannot be mapped onto qualitative difference.

These remarks should not be taken to deny what seems obvious—that people usually derive great pleasure from the music they play and listen to. The proper implication is only that the source of music's value must lie elsewhere. The underlying idea is an Aristotelian one—not that there is no relation between music and pleasure, but that the relationship is the other way round. Great music is neither valuable nor valued because it gives pleasure; rather it gives pleasure precisely because of the great value we attach to it. An alternative, and very familiar, explanation of the value of music appeals to feeling and emotion. This is a long-standing and somewhat vexed topic in the philosophy of music. On the one hand, the precise connection between music and emotion seems impossibly difficult to specify precisely (see Budd 1985). Yet the alternative assertion, famously made in Eduard Hanslick's influential essay 'On the Beautiful in Music'—that music has *no* intrinsic relation to emotion—somehow always fails to convince. It seems impossible to deny that there is some essential connection between music and emotion, especially post-Romantic music. What is equally hard to deny, however, is that Hanslick's analysis exposed the deep error in some common lines of thought. It is simplistic to identify emotion in music with episodes in the biography of the composer (Elgar's experience of melancholy in old age, Tchaikovsky's patriotic pride at the defeat of Napoleon, and so on). And the role famously attributed to it by Congreve in the line 'Music hath charms to soothe the savage breast' too easily reduces it to a kind of therapy that could be replaced without loss were more effective therapies to be discovered. Nevertheless, though mistaken views about music and emotion are common, a connection of some sort between the two is so widely assumed by composers, performers, critics, and audiences that the subject warrants closer attention. It is especially worth attention in the present context, because emotion is a much more likely candidate than pleasure as an explanation of how autonomous art music could 're-enchant' a world that religion once enchanted.

CHANTING AND RE-ENCHANTING

It might be thought a failing that the argument of this book should have proceeded so far without any express attention having been given to the concept of 're-enchantment'. On the other hand, because of its etymological connections, the discussion of music rather than the other arts seems the most appropriate point at which to address the concept directly. The dictionary's first definition of 'enchant' is 'to cast a spell on', but the word comes from the Latin *incantare*, which means 'to sing a magic spell over'. This may not seem to help greatly. If religion is dying in the cultures of post-Enlightenment Europe, then magic is already dead, and thus the prospect of making the world magical again is an even more hopeless one than restoring the place of religion. But this is true only if we have a certain conception of magic. Magic can be thought of as a forerunner of medicine and technology, and this is probably how it is most commonly conceived. As such it is to be regarded as a necessarily futile attempt to move directly from human desire to physical effect. Where technology aims to manipulate the world through an understanding of the causal regularities that govern it, magic aims to act directly upon physical forces by means of word and command. This is a double failure; the forces of nature do not understand language, and the magician's best efforts are thwarted by contingency.

Belief in this conception of magic was common in times past, and anyone who turns to charms, spells, and horoscopes as a means of achieving health or happiness continues to believe in it. Interestingly, the errors in magic so conceived were as much the target of religion as of science and technology (see Thomas 1971/1978). But it is not the only conception with which human beings have operated. Wittgenstein observes with respect to some of the magical practices recorded in Fraser's *The Golden Bough* that those who engaged in rain dances and the like also had a perfectly adequate grasp of the mechanics of sowing and reaping, and of the growing seasons. If they danced for rain, therefore, the 'short-cut' interpretation could not be the complete account of what was going on. It is not necessary to go further into the anthropological debate, however. What matters here is not how the 'magical' practices of different societies and cultures are to be understood, but whether there is a conception of something plausibly called 'magic' that might illuminate the topic of re-enchantment.

Such an alternative conception of magic is to be found in R. G. Collingwood's *Principles of Art* (1938/1974), a major work in twentieth-century philosophical aesthetics, whose third chapter is entitled 'Art as Magic'. As Collingwood construes it, the aim of magic is not pseudo-technological manipulation. Rather, magical practices bestow emotional values on the world, and thereby summon up corresponding emotions on the part of people participating in those practices. Such emotional 'colouring' is necessary for the relation between world and action, and it can exist without any deliberate inculcation. A lion can truly be said to be dangerous because it usually, and properly, induces fear in human beings. This is a two-sided relation. In the absence of human beings, lions are not dangerous, but it is not merely human fear that makes them dangerous. That is why fear of spiders, though often real enough, is irrational. Sometimes, though, the world has to be *given* its emotional colour, and this is just what magic (on Collingwood's account) does. Thus, the purpose and effect of a war dance, for example, are to cast opponents in the role of enemy, and to summon up in those who have to fight a corresponding strength of resolve. But, as this example shows, magic does not have to take the form of 'mumbo-jumbo'—that is to say, strange esoteric formulae that are the possession of a special few. Magic has often been like this, certainly, but it need not be.

Another of Collingwood's examples is patriotic song, and this is an example more likely to be illuminating in the contemporary world. At the beginning of international sporting events, it is common for the national anthems of competing teams to be sung. The words and music are intended to summon and direct patriotic feeling, and the aim is to instil both a sense of competition and a sense of national pride. In point of fact, 'official' anthems are not infrequently somewhat dreary, and the effect they are supposed to have is often more powerfully brought about by 'unofficial' anthems. Either way, though, it is the invocation of such feeling that turns a mere game into an international contest, and creates the sort of atmosphere that is quite often described as 'magical'.

Collingwood's non-instrumental conception of magic enables us to sketch a way in which music might enchant the world—by bestowing emotional values upon human experience, and arousing corresponding emotions in those whose experience it. Clearly, functional music can do this, and religious music might be said to do it par excellence. Consider once again the example of the Bach Passions. In these the Evangelist and the chorus tell the story of Christ's trial and death in biblical texts that in Bach's time would have been thoroughly familiar to all those present. The Evangelist's musical line is the least embroidered—for the most part a simple recitative appropriate to narrative. Some choruses add a dramatic element, most famously with the crowd shouting 'Crucify him!'. The effect of the accompanying music, both vocal and instrumental, is to lend the text more intensity than the familiar words themselves can normally be expected to convey. But it is in the arias and chorales (as well as other choruses) that the music's major contribution is to be found. These add nothing to the storyline. They are devotional, both expressing and arousing emotions appropriate to Christian people contemplating yet again the mystery of Christ's passion. The work as a whole thus serves to bestow emotional value on the object contemplated—to make real the experience of 'what Christ has done for me', and to provide a vehicle in which the corresponding emotion of the faithful can find expression.

There are other examples of such 'enchantment' besides religious ones. As the earlier example of sporting contests suggested, national pride and patriotic feeling are obvious instances, and the music of state ceremonies and military bands often plays this role. But all these are cases in which, it seems, the music is both functional and subservient, and thus falls short of the autonomy that Berger thinks art music must have. So the issue to be addressed is whether non-functional art music can also work magic in this sense, or, to put it another way, whether there can be an art music equivalent of a Bach Passion.

MUSIC AND EMOTION

The excursion into Collingwood and magic was prompted by the issue of music's relation to emotion. Collingwood is himself an expressivist, and sees emotion or feeling as crucial to art. Nevertheless, he denies that 'art as magic' is 'art proper', from which it follows that the relation between emotion and 'art proper' must be different. What can it be? Hanslick is surely correct in thinking that there is a problem about attributing emotional states to abstract music. When I listen to a sad song, the music may add emotional intensity, but it is the words that identify the intensified emotion as sadness, and the experiences or thoughts they express that give the sadness an intelligible object. The music without the words may continue to do this by contingent association, but how can abstract music that has no such associations have emotional content? For familiar reasons, neither the composer's psychological history nor the typical audience's reaction provides an adequate explanation (see further Graham 2005).

Both these suggestions share the same presupposition—that the emotions to which music is related must be located beyond the music—and this makes the connection between the two entirely fortuitous. In his book *Music Alone*, Peter Kivy (1991) offers an interesting alternative view—namely, that it is a distinctive feature of abstract music that it provides its own emotional objects. When I find a piece of music exhilarating, there is neither an independently identifiable emotion aroused by the music, nor a non-musical object towards which my emotion is directed. The exhilaration is found in the experience of listening, and it is the music alone that is to be described as exhilarating. This account of the matter successfully accommodates three factors that most other accounts fail to. First, *pace* Hanslick, when people listen to music they often have the sense of an emotional experience and are inclined to describe the music in emotional terms. Second, although emotional terms seem in order, the range customarily attributed to music is extremely limited compared to other contexts. Third, music alone is an entirely abstract medium; it has no *meaning* (in the normal sense of the word). Once we locate the emotion entirely within the experience of music, all these considerations fall into place. People are indeed moved by the experience of hearing music, but only in ways that music itself can be moving.

From the point of view espoused by Berger, an account such as that of Kivy's has the further advantage of construing the relation between music and emotion in a way that does not compromise music's autonomy. But, by the very same token, it seems that art music cannot enchant. Its inability to do so arises from two features, first its abstractness, and secondly its primarily Apollonian character. The first of these features means that art music cannot give the wider world emotional colouring, because it has no referential relation to that world. This is a crucial point of contrast with music that accompanies words. Bach's Passions intensify religious emotions, but the emotions themselves are roused by and focused upon the story of Christ's Crucifixion. National anthems raise patriotic fervour, but only because they are identified independently with the countries of those who sing them. Without such external reference, the emotional experiences generated by music, even though described as emotional, are *sui generis* and refer us to nothing beyond themselves. This is how they should be, from a point of view like Berger's, and there is no reason for those who think in this way to lament the inability of music to re-enchant the world. In the present context, however, this inability suggests that art music has a crucial limitation.

This limitation need not be fatal, however. The argument of the last few paragraphs has drawn upon the familiar contrast between abstract music and music with words, but it is to be observed that music's power to give the world emotional colour does not have to rely on words. Film scores often contribute emotional colouring to the cinema-goer's experience by means of the visual images that are presented simultaneously with the music; consider how powerful music can be in horror films. A further possibility is context; consider how funeral marches can express and intensify a sense of grief and loss, even though they are accompanied by neither words nor images. Actually, in the case of religion, context can play as important a role as words in enabling music to bestow emotional value on experience. A very large number of organ pieces, for example, have the effect they do because they are played in a church and in a liturgical context.

One conclusion we might draw from this is that, while music alone may not be able to re-enchant the world, it may nonetheless have a role to play, if only the right words, images, and context can be found to accompany it. Of course, this raises the question of what these (so to speak) post-Nietzschean words, images, and context might be, but, before this question can be addressed (as it will be in Chapter 7), there is a residual issue about music. Would music, so deployed, not have lost its autonomy, no longer 'heard for its own sake' and 'nothing but a means of some other practice', to quote Berger again? Here, however, the Dionysian aspect of music that the idea of 'art music' tends to neglect can be called upon to considerable effect.

Collingwood denies 'art as magic' the status of 'art proper' on grounds somewhat similar to Berger's. The power and value of the music that accompanies a war dance must show itself in something non-musical—namely, the consequential heroism of the warriors. If no such effect follows, the music has no value, but any adequate philosophy of art must explain its intrinsic value. However, once we focus on the fact that music is a performing art, the picture changes. It is not just that music leads to activity; it is itself a mode of activity. The point can be made plain by returning to religious music.

Music is often used very effectively to stimulate religious emotion. At evangelical rallies, the organ, orchestra, or choir joins the preacher, and gradually increases in volume as a way of prompting potential converts to get up out of their seats and make their personal pilgrimage to the front of the hall. This, in Collingwood's terms, is music as magic, used here to effective religious purpose. But to suppose that music's role is always external to the action in this way is to overlook another, more common, phenomenon. In the normal case, when a hymn or an anthem is sung, this is not a stimulus to religious action; it is itself a religious act—namely, an act of worship. The activity of praising God does not *follow from* hymn-singing; that is what hymn-singing *is*. The Dionysian character of music lies in its ability to move us to action that is itself musical—namely, playing, singing, and dancing.

It is this Dionysian element that the music of the concert hall suppresses. In a concert performance of a Bach Passion, anyone in the audience who stands up and sings along with the chorales will be regarded as having made a mistake (unless this was part of a deliberate policy of 'audience participation' on the part of the conductor). So would someone who looked for an altar or side chapel in which to kneel, or who lacked any instinct to applaud at the end, or complained that it was in a language he or she could not understand. All these are responses whose appropriateness derives from the contexts of liturgy and church. The concert and the concert hall are different contexts that dictate quite another sort of response.

The implication is clear. If music is to play its part in re-enchanting the world, it must find contexts other than the concert and the concert hall. In the next chapter, we examine the second of these contexts, and explore the possibility of replacing sacred space. In the final chapter, the subject will be the still wider context of a secular alternative to worship and liturgy.

6

Replacing Sacred Space

ART AND ILLOCUTIONARY FORCE

The previous chapter concluded that music's power to enchant the world (by which I mean its ability to give our experience of it an animating emotional colour) depends upon its being accompanied by words and images and set in contexts that, taken together, allow it to have an external reference that music alone cannot have. It does not follow, however, that music thereby loses its autonomy as an art, and becomes a mere instrument by which non-musical ends are to be accomplished. This is chiefly because, being a performing art, music is itself a mode of activity, with the result that human beings can perform actions that are *both* musical and *something more than* musical. The plainest example of this is dance. Dance necessarily involves movement that is not itself music-making. Yet, dance music is more than merely the accompaniment to this movement; without the music the movement would not constitute a dance. A similar point can be made about singing. Words and music are both intrinsic to song, and a singer is not a musician whose instrument happens to be the human voice, but someone engaged in an activity—singing—in which music, words, and bodily movements are inextricably intertwined.

Both dancing and singing can have purposes external to them. Collingwood's example of a war dance is an instance of the first. The purpose of the dance is to engender feelings of a certain kind in those who dance it, and, if these feelings are not forthcoming, the dance has failed. Similarly, before the existence of public address systems, town criers used singing as the most efficient way of conveying information to passers-by. Once more efficient means had been invented, the town crier became a historical curiosity or tourist attraction. In both cases, the dancing and the singing are means to an independently specifiable end. By contrast, on other occasions human beings engage in these activities for their own sake. When they do, singing and dancing (though not confined to 'high' art) have the sort of autonomy that Berger (2002) thinks essential to art in general and music in particular.

For present purposes, however, the greatest interest attaches to a third possibility, one that falls somewhere between these first two. Consider the episode recorded in the Second Book of Samuel, the procession of the Ark of the Covenant when David 'leapt and danced before the Lord' to the sound of horns. In this instance, there is an action whose proper description locates its meaning beyond the relatively simple activities of music and dance. Yet it would be a mistake to regard the dancing and horn-blowing as merely instrumental. David's worship of God was not an end to which the means were music and dance. Rather, these are the (characteristic) modes by which his end was realized. The difference is something like the distinction J. L. Austin (1961) drew between 'perlocutionary' and 'illocutionary' force. The perlocutionary force of an utterance lies in its consequences; the illocutionary force in what it accomplishes intrinsically. Warning someone is (normally) the perlocutionary force of saying 'Look out!'. Naming a child is the illocutionary force of saying 'We will call him Samuel'. In something of the same spirit, we could say that the war dance's perlocutionary force (if successful) is bravery; David's dancing in front of the Ark of the Covenant has the illocutionary force of divine worship, because there are no *external* conditions of success.

The identification of this 'illocutionary' possibility provides a useful way of specifying what it is that the arts must do to re-enchant the world. Previous chapters on the visual arts and literature found that the aspiration to artistic self-consciousness, which the autonomy of art seems to require, falters in a combination of passive aestheticism and cultural insularity. But what finally emerges from the discussion of music is the prospect of combining these arts in a way that breaks through this insularity without relinquishing the aspiration to autonomy. This conclusion flows from a detailed consideration of the use of music in religious worship, and in particular the great works of Bach as vehicles of penitential devotion. Treated merely as a work in the musical canon, the *St Matthew Passion* can certainly be an object of great beauty, one that invariably wins our contemplative admiration, and it may, furthermore, generate the sort of emotional experience peculiar to music alone. Both properties explain why the work continues to be valued by auditors to whom its theological content means nothing. But this response falls considerably short of a religious apprehension of the work, and hence far short of the purpose for which it was created.

The crucial difference cannot be words or music, however, since between liturgical use and concert performance these remain the same. Accordingly, it is the context that matters. This context has two aspects. One is place—church rather than concert hall. The other is occasion—the observance of Good Friday rather than simply a recital in a season of concerts. We might characterize these two contextual differences by saying, first, that the *St Matthew* was written for performance, not just anywhere, but in a 'sacred space', and, second, that it was meant, not just for any convenient time, but for a specific religious 'festival'. I shall use both expressions in this chapter and the next to explore the issue of context. The purpose of this chapter is to investigate secular alternatives to sacred space, and of the next to look at secular alternatives to festival.

HOLY PLACES AND SACRED SPACES

It is notoriously difficult to characterize religion in a way that will encompass all the phenomena that fall under that label. Some religions are profusely polytheistic, others strictly monotheistic. Some are highly sacramental, others stress mystical experience. Still others are chiefly concerned with the regulation of daily life. Some have an associated theology of great complexity, some only a few simple concepts and ideas. But, in all this vast variety, at least two features seem universal—rituals and special places. Every variety of every religion prescribes specific forms of action that are to be repeated on a regular basis and whose ultimate meaning does not lie in their causal efficacy (though often it is partially understood in this way). And always there are prescribed places for these actions to be performed. The contrasts, even within one religion, are very great, it is true. Christianity, for example, encompasses the Eastern Orthodox Liturgy of St John Chrysostom, conducted with rich harmonies and elaborate ceremony in ornate buildings, and also the silent Quaker meeting in a sparsely furnished Meeting House. Yet, despite their evident differences, both are accurately described as ritual acts in special places.

Rituals are actions of a distinctive kind. In a previous chapter I argued that the inspiration to action is a special difficulty both for Surrealism's attempt to 'see the sacred' in a post-religious way, and for literature's efforts to lend a non-cosmic narrative structure to the lives of individuals. It is not so hard to understand how visual and literary art can provide 'epiphanic moments'—that is, experiences that generate a 'sense of something far more deeply interfused' (as Wordsworth puts it). The problem is to connect those moments with action. In what way would art's re-enchanting the world make a difference to how we live? The fact of art's having won its autonomy from religion in the way that it has creates an obstacle to its replicating the accompanying actions that it has left behind. In the main, these actions are those of ritual, and ritual is a subject to be returned to.

For the moment, though, it is enough to observe that the ritual actions of religion are very often performed in special locations. Of these special locations we can distinguish two kinds—holy places and sacred spaces. By holy places I mean specific geographical locations. Generally speaking, the holiness of such places arises in one of two ways. Either they have the reputation of possessing a special numinousness, where, so to speak, the veil between this and another world is especially thin, or they are places associated with events of great importance to the religion in question. The Seven Sacred Rivers of Hinduism and Mount Athos in Greece (whose name is Holy Mountain) are examples of the first kind; Mount Sinai, where Moses received the Ten Commandments, and Golgotha the place of Christ's crucifixion, are examples of the second, as are the numerous places where cuttings of the Bo tree grow—that is, the tree under which Gautama the Buddha was first enlightened. Many of these holy places are the focus of major acts of pilgrimage. A pilgrimage to Mecca is one of the Five Pillars of Islam, and Kasi on the Ganges is of such importance that pilgrimage to it secures perpetual bliss for any Hindu who dies there. Other holy places are important for specific purposes—Lourdes as a place of healing, for instance—and some are the exclusive site for ritual actions performable only at that place, as temple worship at Jerusalem was for Judaism before the destruction of the Temple in AD 70.

Complementary to these holy places are a second kind of special location—sacred spaces. These are spaces intentionally set apart for religious purposes, and their religious significance arises from their being devoted to this use. It is not essential that such sacred spaces take the form of buildings or that they even be permanent; in some religions caves are reserved as places of worship, and both the Muslim's prayer mat and the travelling preacher's tent are sacred spaces. The vast majority of sacred spaces are not as transient as these, however, but buildings intended to last, if only for a few generations. It is with religious buildings that I shall be chiefly concerned, because they are (usually) works of architecture, and architecture is another of the arts.

Churches, temples, mosques, synagogues, and shrines all fall into the category of enduring sacred spaces, deliberately built as such, and in many instances publicly set apart through a ritual act. A very large number (probably the majority) of Christian churches have been ritualistically consecrated—that is, *made* sacred—and have to be ritualistically deconsecrated when they are no longer used for religious purposes. Likewise, the Qur'ān (124.36) expressly mentions 'houses which God has allowed to be built, that his name may be spoken in them', with the result that mosques can claim Koranic blessing and thus be sacred spaces. Explicit acts of consecration are not essential, however. A building becomes a sacred space simply by being set aside, whether temporarily or permanently, as a place whose special purpose is to provide for religious action of some sort—prayer, sacrifice, homage, liturgy, homily, and so on.

Holy places and sacred spaces are not mutually exclusive. The latter may be made out of the former. The Mosque of the Prophet at Medina is a holy place as well as a sacred space, since it was there that Muhammad for the first time prayed facing Mecca instead of Jerusalem; the Church of the Holy Sepulchre stands on the site of the tomb where, tradition holds, the body of Jesus was laid. But, though their location may coincide, holy places and sacred spaces are conceptually distinct.

The distinction is crucial for present purposes, because a defining characteristic of an irreligious world is that it has no use for the concept of 'the holy', and thus for holy places. Nietzsche's declaration that 'God is dead' strikes at the heart of monotheism, and Judaeo-Christianity in particular, but an irreligious world has dispensed with more than the Judaeo-Christian God. Like some varieties of Buddhism, it has no use for 'gods' of any kind, but, unlike Buddhism, it has also discarded the supernatural as such. The concept of a holy place is one where, as I expressed it earlier, the veil between this and another world is specially thin. For the secular world there is no other world, only this one. That is why secular humanism cannot have any equivalent of the holy places that religions typically venerate.

The idea of the holy, and related concepts such as piety and worship, will be returned to at the start of the next chapter. For the moment, it is enough to note that the impossibility of any secular equivalent to holy places does not in itself imply that there can be no equivalent of a sacred space. In fact, we could invent a term for them—enchanted spaces—that is, places set aside and reserved for special actions and occasions that are the secular world's naturalistic counterpart to worship and sacrifice. Perhaps indeed, enchanted spaces already exist—the galleries, concert halls, museums, and theatres reserved exclusively for exercises in the arts. But, to decide whether such places truly are equivalents, something more needs to be said about the more familiar sacred spaces of church, mosque, and temple.

A relevant preliminary observation is this. Very many sacred spaces (by which I shall henceforth mean religious buildings) are themselves aesthetically noteworthy. Asked to name a few of the world's greatest architectural works, alongside such glories as Versailles, the Winter Palace, and the Alhambra, most people (who know of them) would include St Peter's Basilica in Rome, Angkor Wat, the Dome of the Rock in Jerusalem, and one or more of the Gothic cathedrals of Northern Europe. This fact raises a question. Is the architectural excellence of such buildings related to their being sacred spaces, and if so how?

One possibility is that there is *no* relation other than a purely contingent one. It is evident why a building that has been set apart for sacred actions, or to house sacred relics or artefacts, should be described as sacred space. The sacredness of the building is by association, we might say. Yet, in the greatest religious buildings of the world, there seems to be a closer relationship than this. Somehow, just as the music of a hymn or a motet is intrinsically connected to its being a song of praise, the architecture of the building and its religious function are more than fortuitously associated. But how? To answer this question it is necessary to look more closely at the artistic nature of architecture in general.

THE ART OF ARCHITECTURE

In the opening paragraph of *An Outline of European Architecture*, Nikolaus Pevsner (1963) remarks: 'A bicycle shed is a building;

Lincoln Cathedral is a piece of architecture.' This succinctly captures an intuitive distinction between architecture and what the Modernist architect Le Corbusier called 'mere' building. But, though the distinction is easily stated, it is much harder to explain. Where exactly does the difference lie? Pevsner himself goes on to say this. 'Nearly everything that encloses space on a scale sufficient for a human being to move in is a building; the term architecture applies only to buildings designed with a view to aesthetic appeal' (Pevsner 1963: 15). By itself this answer simply shifts the question. Where is it precisely that aesthetic appeal resides? Pevsner identifies three dimensions. First there is appearance—the style of window, the rooms' proportions, the internal and external ornamentation, and so on. Second, there is the shape and volume of the building as a whole. Third, there is the treatment of the space within. The first, he says, is the painter's perspective and the second the sculptor's, so it is the third—the treatment of space—that is peculiar to the architect. But this dimension cannot be isolated, and is therefore insufficient on its own to constitute architecture. Surface, shape, and volume also matter. 'Thus,' Pevsner concludes, 'architecture is the most comprehensive of all the visual arts and has a right to claim superiority over all the others' (ibid.16).

This claim, however, is not as impressive as it seems. Since, on Pevsner's account, the three dimensions are all aspects of the visual, the artistic value of the building lies in the ability of its visual aspects to cause 'aesthetic sensations'. In effect, it is how Lincoln Cathedral *looks* that marks it off from the bicycle shed. Now, as a conception of the aesthetics of architecture, this faces the objection that it reduces even the greatest of buildings to a 'decorated shed', to employ a useful expression first coined by the architect Robert Venturi, and put to effective use by Karstin Harries (1997) in his book *The Ethical Function of Architecture*. One problem with the 'decorated-shed' conception is that it breaks the art of architecture into two distinct activities—structural engineering and aesthetic decoration. But, in addition, by confining architectural merit to the aesthetic appeal of the visual impact of a building, it excludes from the critical assessment of a building's merits the very aspect that appears to be essential—namely, function. The strange implication of focusing on 'aesthetic sensations' is that the judgement of a building's architectural merits is ultimately a matter to be decided by those who *view* it, rather than those who *use* it. Yet, if successful or unsuccessful functioning is coincidental, then, *contra* Pevsner's earlier remark, a work of architecture is indeed no more than a work of sculpture 'on a scale sufficient for a human being to move in'. This can scarcely be right. The ruins of the abbey at Rievaulx can have a very powerful visual impact on anyone wandering among them in terms of style, shape, and space. Since these are *ruins*, however, visual impact cannot be enough to make it a satisfactory work of architecture, and would never have been enough, even had it been intentionally designed that way.

This odd result comes about because of Pevsner's account of what makes architecture art. By classifying it as one of the *visual* arts (albeit the greatest of them), in effect he denies any aesthetic significance to its functionalism. By implication he excludes practicality from any assessment of a work of architecture's success. In one way, this is hardly surprising. A central part of the Kantian aesthetic to which Pevsner implicitly subscribes is the idea that art has purposefulness, but not purpose. Since purpose or function is indispensable with respect to building, the application of the Kantian (or Apollonian) aesthetic to architecture means either that architecture necessarily cannot count as an art, or that we must accept a radical division between how well a building performs its function (its properties as a shed) and how well it looks (its decorative features).

Neither horn of this dilemma is attractive. Common usage, as well as intuition, ranks great architects such as Wren and Brunelleschi alongside great composers, painters, and writers. In the face of such usage, and the intuitive conviction underlying it, denying architecture the status of an art altogether looks like an implausible extreme to which we are driven by theoretical commitment. On the other hand, to accord architecture the status of a visual art, even (as Pevsner does) the supreme visual art, means the architect is essentially a decorator rather than an engineer, a creator of appearances not a contriver of practical solutions. The difficulty with this is that, while ornamentation and façade are certainly familiar and important features of some very fine buildings, they can hardly be regarded as the core of the architect's work. It seems obvious that ornamentation and decoration are things that can be added after the work of building has been completed.

If neither horn is acceptable, however, the only solution is to reject the conception that generates the dilemma. In other words, instead of excluding architecture from the realms of art, or confining its artistic aspirations to just one aspect of the architect's work, we should reason the other way about. Precisely *because* it cannot satisfactorily encompass architecture, we should reject the conception of art that gives principal importance to aesthetic sensation stimulated by visual appearance and spatial effect. This means finding a way in which to acknowledge that architecture must be *equally* concerned with form, function, and construction. We need an aesthetic conception that lends importance to all three when assessing the artistic merits of a building that is to be accorded the status of architecture. How is this to be done?

The unsatisfactory concept of the 'decorated shed' arises from the same Kantian or Apollonian aesthetic that Nietzsche rejected with respect to music. The heart of Nietzsche's objection is that an Apollonian absorption in image overlooks the Dionysian impulse to participation. This Apollonian emphasis thus subtly converts the activity of music-making into the contemplation of 'sonic' objects, an aural equivalent of visual art. In something like the same fashion, applied to architecture this exclusive emphasis on appearance inevitably excludes reference to use. Though architecture is not a performing art and thus cannot quite have a Dionysian element, there is nonetheless something of a counterpart, which I shall call 'appropriation'. The idea is that, just as music's power lies in its ability to stimulate our practical engagement, so the art of architecture can enable and prompt us to appropriate the building for practical use.

APPROPRIATING SPACE

Actually, though the arts of music and architecture seem very different, the perception of a commonality between the two is long-standing. It was Schelling who first described architecture as 'frozen music', though there is much to be said for Roger Scruton's observation that it might be more accurate to describe music as 'fluent architecture' (Scruton 2006). One aspect of this commonality is that performance and appropriation are not so far apart, as my formulation with its double reference to the 'practical' suggests. By taking up a song to sing or piece to play, I appropriate it by making it part of *my* repertoire. And, if the song I sing is one of the lullabies I use to put my child to sleep, then my appropriation of the music is in the fullest sense practical. At the same time, importantly it is still an engagement with music. Lullabies do not stand in relation to sleep as narcotics do, and part of the difference is that their words and melodies have fittingness as well as causal efficacy (when they do). The same point can be made about love songs, as contrasted with love 'potions' (if there are such things).

There are musical properties, then, that enable us to appropriate the musical entities that possess them for certain purposes. This is why a funeral march is not suitable for a wedding procession. Similarly, there are architectural properties that better enable us to appropriate the buildings that have them for the purposes those buildings are intended to serve. Consider this example. The function of a house is to be a home. Among other things, this requires it to be wind- and water-tight, to offer protection from cold and heat as well as from dirt and noise, to give a measure of privacy, and to provide for a number of distinguishable activities—sitting, eating, sleeping, bathing, cooking, and so on. Almost all purpose-built houses do this, but we can still draw a distinction between those that can be described as 'homely' and those that cannot. This is not a matter of mere functionality; human ingenuity can make even relatively inhospitable spaces into adequate dwelling places. In a manner closely connected with Collingwood's account of magic, what 'homeliness' adds to a house is a 'feel' to the building that both inclines us and makes it easier for us to make our home there. 'Homeliness' can be added by the activities of the homemaker in furnishing, decoration, and so on, but it can also derive from the house's proportions, internal organization, and external appearance. When this is the case we have reason to describe the architecture of the house as fitting and not merely as serving its function, or, perhaps more accurately, as serving its function in part through fittingness. As a result, the house looks like what it ought to be—a good place to live. One result, often, is that the homeowner is not merely comfortable in it, but proud of it also.

This analysis of domestic architecture enables us now to say something about the construction of sacred space. Sacred spaces serve religious purposes. These purposes can vary considerably. The great cathedrals of Christianity reflect their use for sacrament, liturgy, pilgrimage, and ceremonial processions. By contrast, the appearance of churches in the Reformed tradition often reflects the centrality to that tradition of preaching and hearing 'the Word'. Mosques and synagogues embody the communal gathering of the faithful for prescribed prayer. Yet, however variable the purpose, it is possible to see that the architecture often does much more than provide attractive decoration to a functional building. It makes the building specially fitted to its function by giving it certain architectural features rather than others. So (to use a somewhat platitudinous example), the soaring spire and vaulted ceiling give the Gothic cathedral a feeling of grandeur amounting almost to transcendence, and thus incline and enable the faithful to find this a place where worship of the divine is easier, since the building itself induces something of the awe that true worship requires. The design of some more modest churches gives them a stillness that makes them specially fitting as places in which to pray. Stained-glass windows let in the light, which is their function, but stained-glass windows do so in a way that gives visual expression to the idea of the worshipper being surrounded by the communion of saints. Many churches are cruciform. The space within them is thus symbolically organized in a way that underlines the message of universal salvation through the Cross. Churches in the Eastern Orthodox tradition are especially notable in their fittedness for purpose, being an architectural realization of the Christian cosmos. The ground plan combines the arms of the cross and the four points of the compass. The cupola that towers above depicts the hierarchy of heaven, while lower levels of decoration tell the Gospel story and portray the saints whose discipleship the faithful worshippers should emulate.

Of course, there are huge numbers of churches and mosques that are simply meeting places. There are others that are both functional and in their way attractive, while nevertheless lacking this extra dimension that I have called 'fittingness'. The same thing can be said about the majority of houses—that they are structurally sound and adequate to the purpose of homemaking, without having any identifiable architectural merit. This is true of most buildings, which is just to say that the vast majority of buildings are 'sheds' with or without attractive decoration. Architecture as an art is an ideal and only occasionally realized within the much more common activity of building. Furthermore, the pursuit of the ideal is no guarantee of success. The history of the self-consciously religious architecture of the nineteenth and twentieth centuries contains plenty of failures, as does the self-conscious pursuit of domestic architecture initiated by Corbusier's conception of 'the House Machine'. Indeed, it can be argued more generally that modern architecture's most spectacular failures are precisely a result of too grand a conception of 'architecture as an art' in the domestic sphere. Far from creating places and spaces that feel good to live in, the construction of tower blocks for mass housing in place of the streets accumulated by the passage of time has compelled large numbers of people to live in a deeply inhospitable built environment. The lamentable consequence of modern architecture's self-consciousness as architecture has been houses, in 'estates', whose collective conception and design positively prevent them from constituting homes. Conversely, many of the most desirable dwelling places, whole towns and villages as well as individual houses, have grown up of their own accord without any deliberate 'architectural' endeavour.

A similar point might be made about churches. The architects of ancient temples, village churches, shrines, and even cathedrals are often quite unknown, if indeed they ever had just one. What this shows is the mistake in thinking that sacred space needs deliberate construction. In a huge number of instances it has come about unselfconsciously, and often in the most satisfactory way. This 'accumulation' arguably provides the necessary condition of a more self-conscious architecture to the same end. The aesthetic and functional sophistication of the Orthodox church is a descendant of much simpler forms and conceptions.

Applied to the idea of 'enchanted space', this thought is salutary because it invites us to wonder whether the need for architecturally constructed 'enchanted space' does not already raise a question mark against it. If there is to be such a thing, perhaps, like the village churches and wayside shrines of Christianity, it will have to arise from a process of accumulation, in which case I should say the prospects for 'enchanted space' are both dim and distant. On the other hand, not all Christian or more generally religious architecture has been cumulative in this sense. There are at least some clear exemplars of the deliberate architectural construction of *sacred* space—that is to say, buildings that expressly employ architectural forms to address liturgical/theological problems while aiming at something new. One very clear instance is St Paul's Cathedral in London, which can serve as a paradigm for further reflection.

Asked to cite a famous architect, the inexpert are most likely to name Christopher Wren. Known from an early age as 'that miracle of youth', Wren was a man of quite exceptional ability, being appointed early in life a professor at Oxford, before abandoning what would probably have been a glittering scientific career to become Surveyor of the King's Buildings. It was a major disaster—the Great Fire of London of 1666—that gave him an exceptional architectural opportunity: to oversee the building of fifty-one city churches and a replacement for the old St Paul's Cathedral. Whereas the old cathedral had been an ecclesiastical accumulation of the kind previously alluded to, Wren's St Paul's was unique in being the first cathedral in the British Isles to be designed, constructed, and seen to completion by a single individual. What is of interest here are the building's distinguishing features. Wren's first design was something like a glorified parish church. This was rejected for being too modest. His next proposal was rejected as being too grand, too 'Romish' in style. What was needed was an *Anglican* cathedral, which (in a phrase of John Donne's) sought to be 'neither a naked nor a painted church', a building with the sort of grandeur appropriate to the Restoration compromise between the post-Reformation Catholicism of Mary Tudor and the Puritan church of Cromwell.

Wren spent thirty-five years on St Paul's. The final outcome was neither the original approved design nor his own first (or last) preference. But, as with his more modest city churches (in the majority of which he was less directly involved), Wren succeeded in giving his cathedral the architectural character appropriate to a distinctive ecclesiastical ideal—a place where equal emphasis was given to pulpit and to altar, and where the sense of God's grandeur would be undeflected by too sensual a magnificence. Just as, in his setting of the St Matthew Passion, Bach gave Lutherans a liturgical expression they could appropriate for their use, so too it was Wren's success in this regard that made it possible for the churchmen of his day, and for the inhabitants of London, to appropriate his building as *their* cathedral. This is what made it an architectural masterpiece.

St Paul's can still impress the tourists of a secular world. But it is in the way that the Egyptian pyramids and the Parthenon do—as astonishing human accomplishments worth preserving for their appearance and historical significance. Such places are 'heritage' sites, not buildings with a function and a purpose. This is because, since the thoroughly secularized mind has no use for places in which to worship God, it cannot find St Paul's a specially fitting place in which to do so. By the same token, it cannot appropriate it as architecture. In a similar fashion, a European might listen to the strange quasi-musical recitations of the Koran that are to be heard in Arabic countries, but only as sonic objects of considerable auditory interest. Of course, Christians of many sorts, and not just Anglicans, can continue to find St Paul's a place of word and sacrament. The question here is how and whether post-Christians might find, or set about constructing, a secular building that was, in some sense, the equivalent of St Paul's.

ENCHANTED SPACE

Always bearing in mind an earlier remark about the penalties of too self-conscious an architecture, what we want to know, then, is whether the art of architecture could be used to create 'enchanted space' for a secular world. It is worth observing at the outset that one reason for the relative rarity of architecture (as opposed to building) is expense. Major works of architecture require a great commitment of resources. That is why (leaving socialist-type housing schemes and corporate headquarters aside) they are almost always special projects of a public or political character—palaces, houses of legislature, law courts, national galleries, and museums, as well as temples, mosques, and churches. This reflects two important aspects of architecture; it is declarative and it is costly. Part of the purpose of an architectural masterpiece is to make a public declaration of the importance of the person or function that the masterpiece is intended to serve, and thereby justify the expenditure of resources required to make it possible. Astonishing buildings can come into existence without these conditions being satisfied. The impressive 'fairy' castles of King Ludwig III of Bavaria are cases in point. But the most famous of these—Neuschwanstein—illustrates that even exceptional beauty and stunning location can be insufficient to counteract an overwhelming impression of architectural 'folly', the grandiose rather than the great.

It is the importance of the State, or the Law, that warrants the cost involved in the architecture that embodies it. The palaces and parliaments of almost all nations are among their grandest buildings, and it is their importance that this grandeur is intended not merely to reflect but to declare. In just the same way, Christians, Buddhists, Muslims, Hindus, and so on have used the architecture of their greatest churches, mosques, and temples to make a public declaration of the importance of giving God the worship he is due, and this justifies the sacrificial expenditure needed to create them. Secular humanists, I have suggested, can 'appreciate' these fine buildings too, but only in an attenuated sense, because they cannot appropriate them to their use. Are there any equivalent buildings that they could appropriate, that would be worthy of similar expenditure, and able to make public declaration of their cost with at least as much hope of justifying it thereby? One thought is that, if we could look to architecture to design and build 'temples of the arts' (a phrase expressly used by Mrs W. K. Vanderbilt for her Marble House in Newport Rhode Island), and to the literary, musical, and visual arts to provide their contents, we would have found the new spaces where the secular world is able to be re-enchanted without any assistance from the supernatural.

Are these new 'enchanted spaces' already in existence, in the innumerable galleries, concert halls, opera houses, museums, and theatres that are such a notable feature of the world's major cities? Such places seem to have two features that are strikingly relevant on this point. First, they are often among the cities' most architecturally significant buildings, and, second, they are reserved exclusively for displays of or exercises in the arts. While, on some understandings, theatres, concert halls, galleries, and so on are places of entertainment, their architecture strongly suggests that there is more to them than this. Cinema complexes and amusement arcades, which unquestionably *are* places of entertainment, never have the aspiration to architectural grandeur that buildings devoted to 'the arts' do. Furthermore, architecture on the scale of the Guggenheim in Bilbao (for example) is immensely more costly than anyone would consider justified for an amusement arcade, and a building such as the Sydney Opera House is a political project because it aspires to being a national emblem. No one would choose a cinema for this role. Of course, it could be the case that these differences reflect nothing more than a cultural prejudice, the sort of prejudice Mill struggles to defend in his ultimately untenable distinction between 'higher' and 'lower' pleasures. But another possibility is that they reveal an aspiration distinctive of the modern world, the desire to create something like an enchanted space or 'temple to the arts'.

If the expression is to be more than a *façon de parler*, what characteristics must a 'temple to the arts' have? The arguments of this chapter enable us to answer this question at least in the abstract. The architecture of a 'temple to the arts' will create a space that both inclines and empowers those who enter it to find, not some 'higher' form of consumer satisfaction, but a mode of activity that, in and for itself, bears constant repetition. This is the counterpart to religious ritual. Furthermore, people's engagement in this activity, in the context it which it most fittingly takes place, will lend meaning to ordinary life beyond the confines of 'the temple', and will do so by giving the activities of ordinary life a certain sort of emotional 'colour'. This is the counterpart to religious faith.

It is not difficult to find familiar ways of speaking about the arts and their institutions that accord reasonably well with this abstract description. For instance, people will say that a concert was 'inspirational' or that visits to art museums enabled them to look at the world with fresh eyes. Perhaps this is just what it is to have the world re-enchanted. Yet there is at least one important element still missing, and once more it is reflected in architecture. This is its communal dimension. So far as it goes, the abstract description that parallels the religious case is compatible with an entirely individualistic 'refreshment', a sort of therapy that helpfully re-enchants my personal world. But, just as the architecture of the great cathedrals and temples makes a public declaration of the importance of the things to which they testify, so the architecture of those buildings we might most readily think of as 'temples to the arts' also places them in the category of 'public' architecture. Personal re-enchantment could arise from reading a book. It could take place in the cinema. By contrast, the public grandeur of the art gallery and opera house suggests that what is in prospect is something more than personal encouragement—namely, the enchantment of the world for the community as a whole. This is why the artist is more than entertainer. He or she speaks not just to individual desire and personal satisfaction, but to, and for, a culture.

Re-enchantment, then, if it is to happen at all, must take place at least in part on a social and cultural level, as well as in the lives of individuals. In the religious case, this communal element is realized in festival, the other element present in virtually all religions. Festivals and observations such as Eid, Diwali, Easter, Hanukkah, Kumbh Mela, Lent, Ramadan, and Yom Kippur, as well as the special character of Friday (Islam), Saturday (Judaism), and Sunday (Christianity), are both central and foundational to the life of the believer. In Christianity, it is precisely for these occasions that the greatest artistic endeavours are made. What this means, in the present context, is that, in addition to ritual and sacred space, any post-Christian re-enchantment will have to find its counterpart to festival. This is the topic of the next chapter, but, since it is also the last, a summary of the argument up to this point may be useful.

THE PROSPECTS FOR RE-ENCHANTMENT

It is to Max Weber that we owe the expression 'the disenchantment of the world'. What Weber was pointing to is a double feature of nineteenth-century developments in Western culture—namely, the decline of religion and the rise of science. In a religiously 'charged' world, such as the world was perceived to be in most times past, and some times present, the character of human experience, animated as it is by the subjective, resonates with the world as it is experienced, since there is (so to speak) a corresponding subjectivity written into the nature of things. When people believe that objective nature is the product of a subjective Being (or beings), then the necessary conditions of a meaningful existence are relatively easily supplied, because human desire and aspiration can aim to fashion themselves around the divine will and eternal purpose of the world. Meaning arises from the natural being brought into conformity with the supernatural. But the increasing intellectual successes of a purely objective form of enquiry and explanation erode this belief. The world becomes a world of 'fact' in itself without meaning. Of course, human desire can, in Hume's expression, 'spread itself upon the world', and thereby bestow value on it. The things around us can be good just because we want them. But, to repeat a distinction I have elaborated elsewhere, value is not the same as meaning (see Graham 2001: ch. 6). The faculty of human desire, unlike that of other animals, is self-conscious, and can ask not only 'what ought I to desire?', but, more devastatingly, 'why is it better to get what I desire than not to desire anything at all?'. In short, while for the most part human beings can just get on with living life, sometimes they need the additional assurance that life is worth living.

From whence is this assurance to come? In so far as science has displaced religion, it has impoverished human life. What we might call pure science is the most cognitively powerful tool the human mind has uncovered (or devised), but the knowledge it produces is not of a kind that allows any place to subjective knowers themselves. This is why (despite frequent pretensions to the contrary on the part of *scientism*) science does not produce the sort of truth that one can live by. What it can do, and manifestly has done, is generate technologies for desire-satisfaction whose power vastly exceeds the techniques that human beings had hitherto laboriously contrived over most of their history. But science can never secure the value of the ends to which these technologies are used. If, as Nietzsche believed, the displacement of religion is permanent, and if the science that has displaced it cannot provide the assurance of meaning that religion formerly did, is such assurance to be found at all? The sense that science's displacement of religion leaves a humanly important 'gap' of some kind is part of what Kolakowski has called 'the revenge of the sacred in the secular' (Kolakowski 1990: essay 6).

Furthermore, it is self-referential. That is to say, the value of science is not something that science can itself explain.

The defeat of Religion by Science is a story by now so familiar that it is widely regarded as incontestably true. And its high degree of abstraction can disguise the fact that it remains a historical hypothesis about cultural and intellectual change. As such it is subject to empirical confirmation or refutation. Yet the true history of 'secularization' is almost impossibly difficult to determine. Its nature, date, extent, and explanation are all topics of enormous complexity and hence continuous and continuing debate. Part of the complexity of the debate arises from its interconnection with another, related, though distinct, debate that is more philosophical than historical. This is the debate about secularism, about whether or not we should regard the decline of religion as an impoverishment or an enrichment of human life. Nietzsche, for whom the demise of religion brought the promise of humanity's final liberation to be itself, its freedom at last to acknowledge, and to celebrate, the 'human, all too human', correctly saw that Religion had informed all thought and culture so deeply and so long that nothing short of a philosophical 'revaluation of all values' would suffice to understand both what its demise meant and where it ought to lead. A premiss of this book is that Weber's question about disenchantment is most profitably explored as part of just such a 'revaluation of all values'.

Alongside the philosophical and historical story of Religion and Science is another—namely, the relation of Religion and Art, which (in Western culture at least) were initially conjoined in a single endeavour. The history of Art is plausibly a history of its struggle for autonomy, and this means in large part autonomy from the religion that gave it its greatest stimulus. Once more a question of impoverishment and enrichment arises. To the extent that it abandons all interest in Religion, is Art better or worse off? One answer (again owing to Nietzsche) is that, far from losing the thing that gives it life, the decline of Religion gives Art its greatest opportunity, to become the means by which humanity can enchant its own world.

In *Gentle Regrets*, a book that in a rather different way is concerned with many of the themes of this one, Roger Scruton describes imagination as 'the precious gift that will re-enchant a disenchanted world' (Scruton 2006: 117). A little later he expands on this to say:

Myths, stories, dramas, music, painting—all have lent themselves to the proof that life is worthwhile, that we are something more than animals, and that our suffering is not the meaningless thing that it might sometimes seem to be, but one stage on the path to redemption. High culture has in this respect been the handmaiden of religion. (ibid.138)

It is plausible to suggest that, just as the sciences are the most fully developed manifestations of human cognition, so the arts are the chief vehicles of human imagination. Is it equally plausible to claim that it is this property that makes them the most promising source of meaning in a wholly naturalized world, no longer the handmaiden of a lost religion, but its substitute? The chapters up to this point have been attempts to assess this claim by looking directly at specific arts, and at those practitioners of them whose ambition in this regard is most evident. In the visual arts it was the Surrealists who made the greatest efforts to enable us to 'see' the sacred, and in literature Joyce provides us with the paradigmatic instance of the life of art preferred to the life of faith. In both, the self-consciousness of the artist seems at one and the same time a necessary precondition of the ambition's realization, and yet the very thing that undermines the cultural connections that would enable it to infuse ordinary life with meaning. In part, this is because its self-consciousness *as art* is so closely tied to a Kantian or Apollonian aesthetic that can sustain only purposeless contemplation.

Nietzsche's criticism of the Apollonian aesthetic is founded on his perception that music cannot properly be made to fit it, despite the recurrent tendency of musicologists and musicians themselves to do so. Attention to religious music of the highest order, however, reveals another possibility—that music is an art that can be functional without loss of autonomy, and this provides a clue to how art's ambition to re-enchant the world might be reconceived. The key is to connect the concepts of performance and appropriation. Performance is a mode of engagement with music as music, and yet through singing and playing we can also appropriate the music to (some) non-musical ends. This is precisely what happens in the religious case. A hymn or anthem does not cease to be music when it is used for the purposes of divine praise. In something like the same way, architectural features do not cease to be products of aesthetic imagination when they serve practical ends. Rather, their ability to serve those ends 'fittingly' is precisely what marks them off from the merely functional. In both cases, what the art in question does is give an emotional 'colouring' to experience that in important ways makes the world 'our' world.

These observations about music and architecture lead to a more general thought. Art can continue to be art without the disfiguring cultural isolation of inward-looking self-consciousness (some would say self-indulgence) that has haunted so much modern art. It can do so, provided it serves the right sort of non-artistic purposes. What can these be? Clearly some things are ruled out—art as design, art as propaganda, for instance, and art as magic (as Collingwood means this). Art as worship is not. Might there be a secular equivalent of this? One answer (which is close to Nietzsche's, I think) conceives of Art as a way of *celebrating* what it is to be human. To explore its adequacy we need to investigate the prospects for 'celebration' on two levels, the social and the individual. On the social level, the idea that suggests itself is the art of festival; on the individual level, Nietzsche directs us to something I shall call the 'dance of life'. These are the themes of the final chapter, but, before returning to them directly, it is necessary to make good on an earlier promise and consider more closely the concept of holiness.

7

The Art of Festival and the Dance of Life

HOLINESS

It is a feature of contemporary English, both British and American, that a range of religious vocabulary is difficult to use in the way it once was. The words 'piety' and 'pious', for example, no longer have the positive connotations that their Latin forebear *pietas* had. A distinction between 'the religious' and 'the religiose' is now hard to draw, 'the saintly' are lumped together with 'the sanctimonious', and the word 'holy' almost always carries an overtone of 'holier-than-thou'. The sole survivor is 'sacred', but arguably in its commonest uses this has no real meaning. It functions simply as a signal that nothing more can be said (or heard) on a particular subject, as, for example, when people declare, in the course of moral argument, that 'life is sacred'. (Several clear, but in my view completely fruitless attempts to give 'the sacred' meaning will be found in Rogers (2004).)

The rejection of these terms with their original connotations is probably a reflection of the degree to which contemporary Western culture is secularized, but the struggle to retain a positively charged religious vocabulary in the face of contemptuous dismissal can be found before the more usual dating of secularization. It is the desire to do so, in fact, that animates Schleiermacher's *On Religion: Speeches to its Cultured Despisers* (1799/1996) referred to briefly in the opening chapter. The highly cultivated Germans and converts of the Enlightenment whom Schleiermacher was addressing held the view that all manifestations of religion are some kind of mental or psychological aberration, too far beneath any serious intellectual engagement to warrant anything more than contempt. This attitude to religion is so familiar an aspect of the contemporary world and so widely regarded as evidence of its distinctively secularized character, it is worth emphasizing the fact that Schleiermacher's *Speeches* were first published in 1799. Their considerable continuing interest, especially in the context of the topics of this book, shows this aspect of 'the modern mind' to be a mistaken self-image of the age.

As is well known, Schleiermacher's short volume inaugurated an apologia for religion that sought to direct attention away both from the Reformation and Counter-Reformation emphasis on theological *belief*, and from the emphasis on moral conduct that had succeeded it. These are 'manifold aberrations; metaphysics and morals have . . . invaded religion on many occasions, and much that belongs to religion has concealed itself in metaphysics or morals under an unseemly form' (Schleiermacher 1799/1996: 19). The cultured despisers, understandably but mistakenly, have dismissed religion by confusing it with either the crude practices of superstition or the arcana of theological-cum-metaphysical speculation, or both. In response, however, the so-called friends of religion have sought to defend it either by embracing a more 'scientifically' acceptable theology, by identifying the ethical as the core of religion, or by talking up religion's social usefulness. This last manœuvre, Schleiermacher thinks, is rightly to be regarded with contempt, but neither of the others is satisfactory either, because both try to convert religion into something different. The key is to focus on religious feeling or sentiment. Only then will we understand, and explain, the distinctiveness of religion, what it is in itself.

Religion maintains its own sphere only by removing itself from the sphere and character of speculation [i.e. metaphysics and theology] as well as from that of praxis [i.e. ethics]. Only when it places itself next to both of them is the common ground perfectly filled out and human nature completed from this dimension. Religion shows itself to you as the necessary and indispensable third next to those two, as their natural counterpart, not slighter in worth and splendour than what you wish of them. (Schleiermacher 1799/1996: 23)

By the same token, however, the assumption of the cultured despisers that science and morality can break free of religion is no less mistaken.

To want to have speculation and praxis without religion is rash arrogance. It is insolent enmity against the gods; it is the unholy sense of Prometheus ... Praxis is an art, speculation is a science, religion is the sensibility and taste for the infinite. Without religion, how can praxis rise above the common circle of adventurous and customary forms? How can speculation become anything better than a stiff and barren skeleton? (ibid.)

At the heart of Schleiermacher's defence of religion and criticism of its opponents is the 'idea of the holy', an expression made famous one hundred years later by Rudolph Otto, the author of a book by that title, and the person also responsible for the centenary republication of the *Speeches*. At an earlier stage, when distinguishing between holy places and sacred spaces, I made the elimination of 'the holy' the definitive characteristic of secular humanism. Whatever form 're-enchantment' may take, it cannot replace religion completely, otherwise it would be its restoration rather than its replacement. One way of specifying the necessarily absent element is to make 'the holy' the distinctive ingredient of religion properly so called. The advantage of this characterization is that it enables us to give a very precise formulation to the question with which this book is concerned, and a clear focus for the remainder of the argument. If secular humanism *necessarily* eliminates 'the holy', then neither art nor any other sphere of human activity can be called upon to make up the deficiency. Yet, to deploy Schleiermacher's language, art might nonetheless provide us with 'the indispensable third', an alternative 'counterpart' that can stand 'next' to science and morality and save them from 'rash arrogance'. To investigate this possibility, we need to know what exactly the elimination of 'the holy' is the elimination of, and one way of doing this is to look at Schleiermacher's account of the 'unholy'.

The 'unholy' for Schleiermacher is the Promethean—that is to say, a conception of the world in which human beings regard themselves as the equals of the 'gods'. In such a world both value and creativity emanate from human beings alone, and this inevitably confines them to the technological and the utilitarian. Accordingly, anyone with 'the sensibility and taste for the infinite' must regard the Promethean conception of the world as profoundly unsatisfying. Schleiermacher's strategy in the *Speeches* is to show the cultured despisers of religion that they too must find it repellent, as a world of dead fact and crude practicality. Having secured this agreement, the concluding step in the argument is to assert that it is only in the restoration of a proper and justified interest in the holy that we can find 'a refuge from the coarse barbarism and the cold earthly sense of the age' (ibid. 10).

But is it? Since Schleiermacher's time 'art' and 'the aesthetic' have increasingly been represented, and viewed, as counterweights to both the technological and the utilitarian. This is a large part of the point of the contrast between 'art' and 'design', and the thought that animates the slogan 'art for art's sake'. Why can art not provide a refuge from 'coarse barbarism' just as good as religion, even though it has nothing to say about the holy? On this precise issue, Schleiermacher himself seems somewhat ambivalent.

I should wish [he says] that I could intuit ever so clearly how the artistic sense, by itself alone, changes into religion . . . the possibility of the matter stands clearly before my eyes, but it must remain a secret from me. . . . Religion and art stand beside one another like two friendly souls whose inner affinity, whether or not they equally surmise it, is nevertheless still unknown to them. (ibid. 68–9)

Though Schleiermacher is uncertain, in combination with some elements in his *Speeches*, the arguments of the preceding chapters can help us make a little more headway. How is it exactly that 'the holy' counters the Promethean tendencies of humanism, and might they be countered in some other way? A key element in Schleiermacher's critique of the Promethean is his appeal to the infinite. 'Humanity is only a middle term between the individual and the One, a resting place on the way to the infinite, and a still higher character would have to be found in the human being than our humanity in order to relate us and our appearance directly to the universe' (ibid. 44). The foundation of all religion is an 'intuition' into the infinite context within which human experience is set, and piety consists in acknowledging both this perspective and the boundaries it necessarily sets. To make 'humanity' the end of everything, therefore, is either to treat the finite as though it were infinite, or to suppose paradoxically that somehow, in contrast to everything else in the world, humanity stands apart from the infinite, that it is both *something* and yet *not part of everything*. The first is the sin of hubris, the second mere incoherence, but either or both constitute the essence of 'unholiness'.

Religion so conceived is not necessarily theistic.

> To have religion means to intuit the universe, and the value of your religion depends upon the manner in which you intuit it, on the principle that you find in its actions. Now if you cannot deny that the idea of God adapts itself to each intuition of the universe, you must also admit that one religion without God can be better than another with God. (ibid. 52)

Though this suggests immense latitude in what we can properly call 'religion', it nonetheless allows us to draw an important distinction, which we might express in this way. Any religion understands human beings to be subservient and inferior to, because dependent upon, a higher realm of being, whether this is conceived as a personal and all-powerful God or not. To think otherwise is to attribute an absurd pre-eminence to humanity within the world as a whole.

True piety is thus a kind of humility. It consists in acknowledging our finitude against the 'intuition' of infinity. Worship springs from a reverence for the mysteries that lie beyond our finitude (including the limits of our understanding), and consists in forms of veneration by which piety and reverence are expressed. Thus, properly understood, religious practices—from the simple laying of flowers on the graves of the dead to the great festivals of the most sophisticated world faiths—are acts of piety and expressions of reverence. Though often confused or mingled with superstition, they have no technological or utilitarian value. In so far as we conceive them to be 'good for' human beings, whether on a cognitive, practical, personal, moral, or social level, we fail to understand their properly religious character and convert religion into either magic or therapy or ethics: 'religious feelings should accompany every human deed like a holy music; we should do everything *with* religion, nothing *because of* religion' (ibid. 30; emphasis added). The rationale of piety and reverence does not lie in the ends they accomplish or in their instrumental value, even when they have some, but in their reflecting the reality of the sacred in its full religious sense. By means of a 'natural intuition' we encounter holy mystery, and that is the sole reason to be reverential in its presence and conduct our lives piously. The 'cultured despisers' Schleiermacher is addressing, like their modern counterparts, hold religion in contempt because they think it to be an unhappy mixture of bogus knowledge and superstitious practice. As heirs of the Enlightenment, or 'rational' people, they cannot lend credit to either. This misidentification is understandable since the proponents of religion so often make out their defence of religion in terms of special knowledge, practical advantage, or moral principle, even when these claims disguise the real intuition that motivates them. Yet *both* parties to this dispute commit a profound error in their failure to understand what really lies at the heart of religion.

Such at any rate is Schleiermacher's view. Though we might dispute certain aspects of it, it captures some important distinctions. In particular it enables us to state clearly a crucial difference between *any* religion, and the rejection of *all* religion. Human beings are part of the natural world, both sides agree. Religion sees a contrast between the finitude of the natural world, and the infinite. The natural is set within the supernatural, so to speak. But what marks human beings out from everything else in the natural world is not an extra spiritual 'stuff' of which they are made that partakes in this 'supernatural realm', but rather the ability to perceive ('intuit') this contrast, and thus to acknowledge the necessity (and appropriateness) of piety and reverence. Despite the huge variety between different traditions, the practices of religion—prayer, praise, sacrifice, and so on—are all to be understood as the vehicles of this acknowledgement.

By contrast, secular humanism explains humanity's limitations, not in terms of subservience to or dependence upon a 'higher' level of existence, but in terms of its brute contingency. Human beings are uniquely self-conscious of their existence, and this self-consciousness leads them to seek some deep reason for their existence that will distinguish them from other existing things. But there is no such reason. Human existence, with all its sophistication, is as much brute fact as the existence of sticks and stones. This is a thought that finds its fullest and most explicit formulation in Existentialism, sometimes expressed in the concept of the 'thrown-ness' of human existence. For humanism there is no supernatural. Human beings 'rise above' the merely natural only in their self-consciousness and freedom, though both of these are themselves products of the natural world, and, in comparison with the higher animals, may in any case be a matter only of degree rather than of kind. Accordingly, and contrary to the claims of some that 'human life' (or just 'life') is sacred, *nothing* is sacred in the proper sense. As noted previously, of course, it does not follow that nothing is of value, but, if nothing is sacred, there is nothing worthy of worship. In worship, the religious mind seeks to 'transcend' the finitude of human existence, including the finitude of the individual life that inevitably ends in death. It does so through a proper acknowledgement of the infinite, conceived in monotheistic traditions as our total dependence on God the creator and sustainer of all that is.

Without God, humanity confronts the sheer contingency of its own existence. Religion is the search for a meaning that cannot be found. If such a search is indeed fruitless, what can humanism offer in its place? Is there a 'secular music' by which our deeds might be accompanied like the 'holy music' Schleiermacher makes central to religion? Interestingly, there is a version of the concept of 'transcendence' that can be invoked in this context. Just as religious 'intuition' does not compel just one attitude and a truly religious person might curse God for his existence rather than bless him, so too apprehension of the brute contingency of our existence can generate any of at least three distinct attitudes. One is religious (or other) pretence—Sartre's 'bad faith'. Another is honest but reluctant acceptance—authenticity. But a third is the pursuit of a distinctively human transcendence, which is to say a way of 'overcoming' the contingency of our existence through the very self-conscious freedom that seems to be threatened by it. This is how I interpret an important strand in Nietzsche's thoughts on this issue, a strand that builds on elements in Schopenhauer's *The World as Will and Idea*.

ART AND TRANSCENDENCE

At this point it is worth repeating Nietzsche's remarks about art and religion.

Art raises its head where religions decline. It takes over a number of feelings and moods produced by religion, clasps them to its heart, and then itself becomes deeper, more soulful, so that it is able to communicate exaltation and enthusiasm which it could not do before. ... growing enlightenment has shaken the dogmas of religion and generated a thorough mistrust of it; therefore feeling, forced out of the religious sphere by enlightenment, throws itself into art. (Nietzsche 1878/2004 150)

In *The Relevance of the Beautiful*, Hans-Georg Gadamer has a related thought about art.

We all know [he says] that visiting a museum . . . or listening to a concert sets a task requiring profound intellectual and spiritual activity . . . . [a]fter going through a museum, we do not leave it with exactly the same feeling about life that we had when we went in. If we really have a genuine experience of art, then the world has become both brighter and less burdensome. (Gadamer 1967/1986: 26)

An experience through which the world becomes 'both brighter and less burdensome' is one interpretation of the ability Nietzsche attributes to post-religious art to 'communicate exaltation and enthusiasm'. Gadamer ascribes this effect to *spiritual* activity, which echoes the same theme. Whatever Gadamer himself may mean by it, for present purposes 'spiritual' cannot be the objective experience of the transcendent or the supernatural, otherwise we would simply have religion by another name. Yet it needs to be something more than a therapeutically valuable psychological boost. If art is to re-enchant the world in the aftermath of religion's demise, it must in some way enable the most honest and truthful apprehension of our finite humanity to be at the same time an inspiration to be human.

A philosopher who might with plausibility be said to articulate just such an idea is Schopenhauer. In *The World as Will and Idea*, Schopenhauer attempts to make good, as he sees it, the crucial deficiency in Kant's philosophy—namely, the necessary postulation of 'things-in-themselves' that are, with equal necessity, unknowable by human beings. According to Schopenhauer, human beings *are* 'things-in-themselves', so that, *pace* Kant, we do have knowledge of 'things-in-themselves', because we have self-knowledge. We know ourselves directly, and not through the representations by means of which we know other things. And what we know is ourselves as sources of will. 'Will' here is to be understood in a rather special sense, not as the faculty by which desire is rationally and hence responsibly controlled, but as the fundamental assertion, affirmation, or drive that makes us living things, and keeps us active while we exist. In this sense, all living things, not just human beings, are manifestations of 'will', which is to say a sort of impulse to life. In plants and other animals, the will is blind; in human beings it is self-consciously apprehended, and, because of this special self-knowledge, we can have insight into the underlying commonality of the 'world as will' that sustains the other beings known to us through representation or perception.

As representations, living things, including ourselves, are instances of universal types, contingent phenomena, distinguished one from another by a *principium individuationis*, and subject to the law of sufficient reason, the law of cause and effect. It is such a law that science formulates, and accordingly science cannot give us knowledge of the universal. Neither does philosophy. It is to art that Schopenhauer thinks we must look for the universal, Platonic 'ideas' that constitute the enduring beings of which the flow of contingent phenomena are manifestations. If we want to apprehend 'humanity' as such, it is fruitless to turn to anthropology or biology. The most these can do is construct laws that generalize over the behaviour of phenomena—that is, historically specific individuals and groups. Universal 'humanity' is to be found in deliberate imaginative representations such as the paintings of the Dutch masters or the plays of Shakespeare, both of them among Schopenhauer's own examples. Unlike a family snapshot, Brueghel's *Country Wedding*, for instance, is not a picture of some particular wedding, but the image of 'a wedding' as such, and Edvard Munch's *The Scream* is not part of a psychiatric record, but an image of the haunted mind (my examples).

Painting, sculpture, and literature at their best enable us to step outside or beyond the *principium individuationis* and give us a transcendent view of human life, indeed of life in general. What we see is that

the world in all the plurality of its parts and forms is the phenomenon, the objectivity of the one will to life. Existence itself, and the kind of existence, both in its totality and in every part comes from the will alone. The will is free; it is almighty. In everything the will appears just as it determines itself, in itself, and outside time. (Schopenhauer 1819/1995: 216)

As 'things-in-themselves' human beings can be directly aware of will, and the peculiar power of music among the arts is to mirror its perpetual striving, and thus give us an immediate apprehension of its activity. One conclusion we might be tempted to draw is that the visual and literary arts provide us with a transcendent perspective by means of which we are best placed to rejoice in our identification with the will to life, while music allows us give joyful voice to this identification. But, famously, Schopenhauer was a pessimist. What we see from this point of view is a cause not for celebration, but for lamentation.

As the will is so is the world. Only this world itself can bear the responsibility for its own existence and nature—no one else bears that responsibility; for how could anyone else have assumed it? If we want to know what people are worth morally, both as a whole and in general, we have only to consider their fate as a whole and in general. This is want, wretchedness, affliction, misery and death. Eternal justice reigns; if they were not as a whole, worthless, their fate, as a whole, would not be so sad. (ibid.)

For Schopenhauer, in the light of this perception, the *affirmation* of the will to live is absurd, and the only satisfactory response to the realization that our individual lives are phenomenal manifestations of the one will is *denial*. Equally well known for his interest in Eastern religion, especially Hinduism, he thus espouses a conception of salvation close to that of *moksha* or escape through annihilation, and in the same spirit commends the tradition of renunciation of the will embodied in Christian asceticism. As the presenter of Ideas, art has its part to play here.

The state in which the character is removed from the power of motives proceeds not directly from the will, but from a changed mode of knowledge. So long as the knowledge is merely that which is entrammelled in the *principium individuationis* and simply follows the principle of sufficient reason, the power of the motives is irresistible. But when the *principium individuationis* is seen through, and when the Ideas, and the inner nature of the thing-in-itself, are directly recognised as the same will in everything, and from this recognition ensues a universal quieter of volition, then the individual motives become ineffective because the mode of knowledge pertaining to them is overshadowed and superseded by a quite different mode, and has passed into abeyance. (ibid. 255)

Whereas the picture we have been working with looks to artistic inspiration to animate more everyday motives to action, Schopenhauer's pessimistic vision of the world requires artistic inspiration to 'quiet' the other motives until all action ceases. The implication cannot be a conception of art that positively enables us to declare 'it's good to be alive', but one that gives greater clarity to the desirability of non-existence. This is the crucial point at which Schopenhauer and Nietzsche differ. For Nietzsche, the supreme achievement in the face of the absence of God and the supernatural, and the perception that humanity is the sole sphere of anything we might call spiritual, is not the denial but the assertion of the will to live, or, in a more familiar Nietzschean phrase, the will to power.

Whether we should follow Schopenhauer or Nietzsche in this is not directly to the point here. Together they allow us to explicate the role of art as the quotation from Gadamer conceives it—a mode of apprehension through which the idea of humanity is presented to humanity itself. In great works of art—visual, plastic, architectural, musical, and literary—we are confronted with the idea of humanity, which is to say 'what we are', and the question for each of us is whether, so confronted, we are able to affirm the will to life in ourselves, and not merely to affirm it, but to celebrate the possibility of its affirmation. This is, I think, the best we can do by way of understanding what it might mean to say that art can re-enchant the world of secular humanism. It remains to ask, however, whether there are modes of activity in which this possibility can be realized.

FESTIVALS

By a somewhat circuitous route, the argument has returned us to the subject of festival. The previous chapter concluded that any post-Christian re-enchantment of the world will have to find its counterpart to the religious festivals of Easter, Passover, and so on. We can now see why. If, as I have put it, the task for art liberated from religion is to provide us with ways in which to 'celebrate the possibility of affirming the will to life', it will most obviously do this in so far as it can provide us with *forms* of celebration, which is to say, festivals. To determine whether art can actually fulfil this task, we need to know what the defining characteristics of festivals are, and how they stand in relation to ordinary life. Gadamer, from whom I quoted briefly, is one of the relatively few modern philosophers to write on this subject. He identifies several important features. First, festivals are essentially communal. This is not to say that they inevitably involve the whole community in a particular locality. It is perfectly possible for individuals to refuse (or just fail) to take part in a festival, and also possible for other people to exclude them on social or ethnic grounds. What is not possible is that individuals (or even groups of individuals) should invent their own festivals (*pace* the US invention of Kwanzaa), or celebrate festivals alone, except in the most attenuated sense. But, while festivals are community events, this is not at all the same as saying that they are state occasions. Sometimes the two combine—as at the time of coronations, perhaps. The crucial difference is this. A state occasion is directed 'from above' while a festival properly so called emanates 'from below'. A state occasion (the May Day parade of the former Soviet Union, for example) is something that large numbers of people may turn out to *watch*; a festival (the Fourth of July in America, for instance) is something in which people *participate*. These particular examples, however, should not lead us to infer that the difference is between the tedious and the enjoyable. In fact the reverse can be true—enjoyable state occasions can come to be preferred to community festivals that have become a bore.

A second, related, feature of festivals is that they are made up of customs fashioned by the accumulation of past practice. That is to say, the pattern of activity festivals prescribe—the way they *ought* to be celebrated—is not one intentionally laid down by official 'organizers', as that of a state occasion or a major sporting event might be. The right way of observing a festival such as Christmas is something embodied in tradition, with no further authority behind it. The only reason to erect and decorate Christmas trees, sing familiar carols, or give each other gifts is that this is what is traditionally done at Christmas time. Furthermore, there is no other way to celebrate Christmas than by doing just such things. Failing to follow tradition is not celebrating Christmas differently, but choosing to spend the holiday period in late December in some alternative way. This relation to tradition applies even to the more detailed religious or public ceremonies that may lie within any particular festival. The 'Festival of Nine Lessons and Carols' for example, is an early twentieth-century innovation, whose invention can be dated fairly precisely. But it became a *constituent* part of the celebration of Christmas only when it took on a 'traditional' character that rendered its intentional invention (and the names of its inventors) irrelevant to its continuance.

The traditional activities that comprise a festival are essentially ritualistic. This does not imply that they amount to little more than the mindless repetition of actions whose meaning and purpose have been forgotten (though sometimes this does happen). Rather, in contrast to most actions, whose rationale derives from their possessing a causal efficacy that can be harnessed to practical ends, the point and purpose of festivals lie in their symbolic meaning. To treat the actions that constitute a festival as practical (in the ordinary sense of the word) is tantamount to thinking that the purpose of a birthday party is to *make* someone a year older. The implication is that, if the actions people perform as part of a festival are to be assessed with a view to amendment, it cannot be with the hope or prospect of making them more efficient. Whereas technologies fall out of use (or ought to) when some better way has been found of achieving the end to which they are employed, festivals die out (or ought to) when they can no longer have the meaning they have hitherto possessed. This is what makes festivals a subject of interest in the present context. An important indication of the decline of religion will be the increasing meaninglessness of the festivals it has hitherto sustained. Arguably, this is what has happened, with Christmas especially. The question is whether Art or the arts can put something more meaningful in its place, and what it would take for this to occur.

One way of expressing the emptiness of Christmas in a secular world is to say that in many places Christmas is no longer *celebrated*; it simply *takes place*. This points us to a third crucial feature of festivals—they are celebratory. Though it may seem like stating the obvious, the celebratory character of festivals is worth drawing attention to, because most societies have important communal events widely observed that are *not* festivals. Armistice Day and Memorial Day, for instance, are annual occasions governed by tradition. Nevertheless, it is only a careless use of language that would speak of them as being 'celebrated' rather than 'kept'. Whatever the language, though, the point is that such solemn occasions ought not to have a *festive* character.

What *is* a festive character? It has at least two aspects. First, a festival must have a celebratory *object*—something to be glad *about*, and second, expressions of this gladness take the form of actions that are unusual in their extravagance. Thus, to take the example of Christmas once more, the traditional object of the festival is the birth of a Saviour. What the festival declares is that humanity is not 'lost', as it might have been. This is the reason for celebration, because it is something to be glad about. Similarly, the Jewish festival of the Passover, while recalling a different story of salvation, is also focused on a cause of gladness—the Jewish people's deliverance from slavery by God, and the start of the journey to a divinely promised homeland. It is the fact that Christmas and the Passover are celebrations that warrant (in biblical language) 'the killing of the fatted calf'. This is the second important aspect of festivity—'pushing the boat out' or a kind of extravagance. Often this takes the form of consumption of food and drink more luxurious, more plentiful, and more expensive than that of other days in the year. The extravagance (in poor societies at any rate) is intensified by the days of celebration themselves being a holiday from the productive labour that daily life requires. This is a further point at which we can see how a festival properly so called might become impossible. A society could become so rich that 'luxurious' food and drink are an everyday occurrence, and levels of economic production so high that holidays constitute no sacrifice. We might call this disenchantment through prosperity—another theme to which there will be reason to return.

A fourth feature of festivals is their timelessness, the characteristic to which Gadamer gives most attention. It is also of special relevance in the present context, because it is the timelessness of festivals that connects them with making human life meaningful, and it is in explaining this that we have reason to invoke the concept of 'transcendence'. The thought is this. Though festivals such as Hanukkah and Diwali take place at a certain time of year, there is also a sense in which they do not take place in time at all. That is to say, they are major occasions, certainly, but not in the way that significant historic events like the French Revolution or the collapse of the Berlin Wall are. One way of expressing this is to say that, rather than being events (major or minor) in the flow of ordinary historical time, festivals provide a high-level framework within which the passage of time can be structured and punctuated and thus made 'practical'. Human beings live *in time*, and not merely (as other animals do) *while time passes*. This requires time to have some structure.

A low-level structuring is made possible by the calendar that is in common use. While the division of time into days reflects a natural phenomenon—the sun's rising and setting—the division into weeks and months does not, and yet such a division is crucial to planned human action. At the same time, one week is indistinguishable from any other. The calendar can be used to date events that then disappear into the past, certainly, but years *as such* follow each other without discrimination. It is an essential function of festivals that, like birthdays, they enable us to cope with the interminable flow of time by bestowing shape and meaning on every year. Thus, we identify the time at which we plan to do things, or recall when we did them, as 'before' or 'after' Christmas, 'at' the Passover, 'during' Ramadan, and so on. As Gadamer puts it: 'We do not describe a festival as a recurring one because we can assign a specific place in time to it, but rather the reverse: the time in which it occurs only arises through the recurrence of the festival itself' (Gadamer 1967/1986: 41).

The Christian calendar provides a particularly clear instance of such temporal structuring. It divides every year into two parts. In the first, the focal point is Christmas, preceded by Advent and followed by the Epiphany. In the second, it is Easter that provides the focus, preceded by Lent and followed by Pentecost. In between these two great cycles lies what the calendar expressly refers to as 'ordinary time'. The crucial point to note, however, is that, although these two cycles mark and celebrate two dateable events—the birth and resurrection of Jesus—and take place in the seasons of winter and spring respectively, the festivals of Christmas and Easter are themselves indifferent to time and date. The year in which they take place is irrelevant.

In summary, festivals may be said to have the following important characteristics. They are communal, traditional, symbolic, celebratory, and atemporal. Now each of these characteristics has an element that it is not fanciful to call 'transcendence'. The communal transcends the individual in just this sense: it provides the individual with the possibility of actions that have form and meaning, but their form and meaning are not the outcome of choice or intention, and in this way they transcend the will of any one individual. The traditional character of these activities allows them to transcend the dictates of contemporary relevance; in whatever period they take place, they have nothing of the nature of 'current affairs'. Their symbolism locates their meaning outside the functional and the instrumentally rational; participation in them is not an achievement or accomplishment of any kind. The celebratory character of festival places it above the order of the everyday, but not by being rare or unusual. On the contrary, nothing takes place with more predictable regularity than Christmas or Diwali. Finally, their atemporality makes them indifferent, not just to date and time, but to the structure of human life itself. Participants in festivals are on an equal footing irrespective of age, and each participation in a festival is of equal significance regardless of the time of life. Playing a piano sonata is an outstanding accomplishment for a 4-year-old, but not for someone at 40. Running a mile is no very great accomplishment for a healthy 20-year-old but is something for an 80-year-old to take pride in. No such comparisons are relevant to festival. While anyone can have a good Christmas or a bad, this has nothing to do with youth or maturity.

Taken in combination, these features give substance to Gadamer's otherwise seemingly extravagant remark that festival is as near as we can come to experiencing eternity. This way of summarizing the transcendent nature of festivals is of special relevance in the present context, because festivals need not be religious. An example that springs to mind is American Thanksgiving. This is not a religious festival (though it often includes some religious observance), but it satisfies all five conditions. Unlike the organized political occasion of the President's State of the Union Address to Congress, Thanksgiving is something that people spontaneously observe across the United States in traditional, time-honoured ways. It has no causal efficacy or practical purpose that might be better served in other ways, but symbolizes for its participants the *unum in pluribus* of America. It does this by having as its focus an event in the mythology of America—its founding and survival—something for which wave after wave of refugees and immigrants have reason to be glad and hence to celebrate. Finally, it is also an event by which the year in the United States is punctuated, something around which personal, public, academic, and business life is arranged.

This is something of an idealization, of course, but the existence and perpetuation of Thanksgiving show that there can be purely secular festivals. At the same time, Thanksgiving would not naturally be described as having 'spiritual' content, and so falls short of what humanistic 're-enchantment' aims at. Perhaps this is because it makes no notable or conspicuous use of art. What needs to be investigated, then, is how the arts could be deployed to add 'spirituality' to a purely secular festival like Thanksgiving, which is to say, enable it to play the sort of role that religious festivals have played in times past (and continue to play in many places, of course).

ART AND FESTIVAL

For the purposes of answering this question, Easter provides a helpful template. The great liturgies of Palm Sunday, Holy Week, and Easter are themselves occasions of music, drama, and visual spectacle, often taking place in awesome architecturally created sacred spaces that were in part intended for them. These liturgies shaped and generated the Mystery Plays of the Middle Ages, dramatic public processions, and Easter 'carols'—that is, popular music with a theological theme—as well as some of the world's greatest works of high art—Leonardo's *Last Supper*, Michelangelo's *Pietà*, Bach's *St Matthew Passion*, the poetry of Donne and Herbert—are among the most notable examples. These great ceremonies and major works spill over into and are connected with a much wider range of activities—family gatherings, feasts, games, recitals, exhibitions, as well as strictly religious observances. Crucially, all these aspects of the festival are held together by a cosmic narrative of death and resurrection, destruction and salvation, a narrative that ties in with the passage from winter to spring, and speaks to the lives of those who celebrate it.

It is this narrative that provides the object of celebration—Christ's victory through suffering over sin and death—a victory that offers everyone the prospect of finding in that iconic suffering the means of his or her own liberation from death's destruction. All the manifestations of the festival derive their symbolic meaning from this object, which thus explains the 'gladness' that a celebratory festival requires. When Easter comes to be observed merely as a holiday, as it has become in many modern societies, the activities it involves lose their meaning. Importantly, this is not the same as saying that they lose their value. On the contrary, the activities tradition prescribes may continue to be valued. Accordingly, Easter Day can remain a date in the diary when extended families make a special effort to get together and to share a meal in which (say) roast lamb, simnel cake, and chocolate eggs figure on the menu. The fact that none of the participants thinks of this as a celebration of cosmic victory and a source of spiritual hope does not prevent them from finding it all an enjoyable and satisfying occasion.

Furthermore, the traditional religious ceremonies might even play a part in this. It is not difficult to imagine such people on (what happens to be) Good Friday giving rapt attention to a performance of Bach's *St Matthew Passion* in an architecturally glorious church, or attending the Easter Day service and being powerfully moved when (as is the tradition in some places) the brass and percussion reach a crescendo before the crowded company sings 'Jesus Christ is risen today'. For the unbeliever, of course, Jesus Christ is *not* risen, today or any other day, so that, while such moments can move secularists quite deeply, the emotional experience does not actually *mean* anything. This is what prevents it from being an experience of transcendence in the sense analysed above. Schleiermacher makes much of feeling as the essence of religion, but this can be misunderstood. The 'feeling' he refers to is not a 'lump-in-the-throat'-type feeling, but an 'intuition' into the nature of the human condition, an apprehension of the finitude of humanity. 'Feeling' in the ordinary sense, such as even the most convinced atheist can sometimes experience at a children's nativity play, leaves us confined to the particularity and contingency of our individual existence; even if we are inclined to treasure it, it is just one more moment in the general flow of experience, merely an episode in the passage of time.

We are still in search of something more, therefore, but we have at least a better indication of what it might be. If art could replace the Good Friday Passion, the Easter anthems, or the Nativity play with an alternative, non-supernatural, yet celebratory object, we should then perhaps have found a way in which the communal actions of individuals might be focused into a festival in the right way. It is not difficult to state such an object in the abstract—namely our membership of the human race. The religious impulse often arises from an anxiety that we are 'alone in the world', and a consequent relief at finding there are other spiritual agencies besides ourselves (the gods, or God and His angels). Wiser and more powerful than ourselves, they are willing and able to direct, save, and redeem us. It is their very existence that calls forth prayer and sacrifice, and their redemptive action that provides cause for celebration. The humanist alternative seems clear. Since there are no such other agencies, we have to accept the fact that, spiritually speaking, humanity *is* alone in the world. Can we go further than acknowledgement and *celebrate* this fact? If we can, we have found (in line with Chapter 1) a source of inspiration that will animate the secondary motivations of work, enjoyment, and belonging. We have also found a role for festival—a communal celebration of being human that can be both focused by and expressed through the arts. The question then is how the fact of our humanity can in itself be a cause of celebration rather than simple acceptance, or, worse, shame and anxiety.

This brings us back to Nietzsche. His objection to all religions, but Judaeo-Christianity especially, is that they are life denying, rather than life affirming. That is to say, far from encouraging us to celebrate our existence as human beings, they invite us to lament it. Having induced us to loathe who we are, they then hold out the promise of some spiritual transformation—a moment or process when (in the words of St Paul) we will all be changed. But the promise is false, because God is dead. It is one thing to grasp this truth as a matter of metaphysics. It is another to live by what it implies—that we have only ourselves to rely on, and must find ways of wholeheartedly endorsing the fact that we are 'human, all too human'. If, as Nietzsche contends, 'growing enlightenment has shaken the dogmas of religion and generated a thorough mistrust of it', and if 'feeling, forced out of the religious sphere by enlightenment, throws itself into art', then it is to art that we must turn for the means of that endorsement. But 'What do all our art of artworks matter if we lose that higher art, the art of festivals?' (Nietzsche 1887/2001: 89).

HUMAN SACRIFICE

It is in *The Birth of Tragedy* that Nietzsche elaborates the distinction upon which the argument of previous chapters turned—namely, that between the Apollonian and Dionysian aspects of art. The distinction is drawn, however, in the broader context of examining the nature and (as Nietzsche sees it) decline of ancient Greek tragedy. Part of this decline is a transformation of the tragedies from religious festival to dramatic production. A key element in this transformation is a change in the main protagonists from 'roles' to 'characters', the former played behind masks, the latter undertaken by actors in their own person. A further element that Nietzsche wants to emphasize (hence the importance of his famous distinction) is the elimination of music, and the chanting of the Chorus in particular. It does not matter for present purposes whether Nietzsche's account of this transformation is historically accurate or not. We can still see how the emergence of music, drama, and dance as distinct arts could signal the demise of the festival in which they had previously been bound together. This festival, though religious, was pre-Christian. Perhaps, then, it may give us a clue about what a post-Christian festival might look like.

Nietzsche wrote *The Birth of Tragedy* at a time when he still admired Wagner, and in it he heralds Wagner as someone who has found a way in which the arts might once more combine to something like the effect with which the ancients had combined them. As is well known, this estimation was to change radically, but there remains something to be learned from Wagner along these lines. Wagner is the master of the nineteenth-century conception of the *Gesamtkunstwerk*—a work of art in which the power of music, drama, and the visual are brought together on a spectacular scale within a mythologically inspired narrative. Furthermore, Wagner himself embraced the sort of ambition for art that it is the aim of this book to explore. In *Death-Devoted Heart*, Roger Scruton quotes this passage from Wagner's writings.

It is reserved for art to salvage the kernel of religion, inasmuch as the mythical images which religion would wish to be believed as true are apprehended in art for their symbolic value, and through ideal representation of those symbols art reveals the concealed deep truth within them. (quoted in Scruton 2004: 7)

Scruton goes on to make a persuasive case for thinking that in *Tristan and Isolde* Wagner 'attempts to articulate the idea of redemption in artistic and dramatic form'. But being, as Scruton alleges, 'one of the great humanists of modern times', Wagner 'recognized humanity's religious need and tried to make man his own redeemer, so as to ennoble the human beyond the divine' (ibid.). This eloquently captures the whole aim of re-enchantment—to conceive of humanity and the human condition in such a way as to make man his own redeemer and thus ennoble the human in the absence of the divine. At the heart of Wagner's opera we find a recurrent religious concept—namely, sacrifice. In this the drama mirrors that of Easter—but with a crucial change. Instead of God's sacrifice for humanity, the focus is on human sacrifice for its own sake. The *Gesamtkunstwerk* unites the various arts in the creation of a single image in which death is chosen, not for some higher purpose that serves the future or the lives of others, but as the supreme expression of self-mastery. It is a fact about human beings that they must die. 'O let my soul live', the Psalmist cries to God, 'and I will praise thee.' When there is no God with whom to plead, and none to praise, the fact of death remains, and the longing for salvation must find some other outlet.

Here we return to one of the themes of Chapter 1. Human beings are embodied spirits, and the fulfilment of their spiritual nature is their self-realization. They need not rest content with mere existence comparable to the existences of plants and animals (though many do, perhaps), but can aspire to a 'life' of their own choosing, can aim self-consciously to *be* someone. As the products of evolution no different from all other living things, they are driven on from moment to moment by something like Schopenhauer's 'will', and the mortality they share guarantees that all their striving will ultimately be extinguished. The difference lies in the fact that human self-consciousness brings the awareness that this is so. The combination of will and self-consciousness generates the paradox of the human condition. We are driven to have hopes that we know will always be frustrated.

For Schopenhauer the only escape is in asceticism—the disciplined suppression of the will to the point where all desire to live has been abandoned. The alternative, exemplified in Wagnerian opera, is the heroic embrace of death. This seizes on a possibility that is unique to human beings precisely because of their freedom and self-consciousness—that they should not merely deny or suppress the will to life, but voluntarily *renounce* it in a supreme act of self-realization.

This heroic alternative needs to be stated with care. It is not instanced in the person who 'lays down his life' for his country, or for his friend. However morally admirable, both are cases in which death is chosen as a means to life. Nor is it realized in suicide as such, which may be nothing more than escape. The heroic response to existence aims to *transcend* the will to life, which is to say, rise above its dictates. One way of bringing this out is to say that heroic renunciation is focused on what is worth dying for, not on what is worth living for. More exactly, its focus is on how death can be made life's crowning achievement. All this must be cast, of course, within a humanist frame. The Christian martyr sacrifices this life in the hope of another, and thus believes that the right kind of death will be followed by resurrection, 'through Jesus Christ, Our Lord'. Such martyrdom is to be found in other religions too. But for humanism the meaning of sacrificial death must lie in transcendence *without* resurrection, and this is the conception that Wagnerian opera aims to depict. 'The Wagnerian hero', Scruton remarks, 'had to be both plausible as a modern human being and at the same time exemplary, setting a pattern of action that instils a renewed sense of human life and purpose' (Scruton 2004: 8).

Wagner conceived his artistic endeavours on the grandest of scales, and famously even built his own festival theatre—at Bayreuth—in which to produce them. 'Festivals' have continued to be held there annually, and it is not implausible to regard the whole phenomenon as the best example to date in which sacred space has been replaced by an enchanted space, and with expenditure on the scale of the truly celebratory, the musical, dramatic, and visual arts combined in a strictly humanistic festival. But just how close does the Wagnerian spectacle come to the great religious festivals? One relevant question is whether both the event and the space in which it takes place can be replicated. That is to say, is Bayreuth truly a repeatable enchanted space that is primarily an exemplar for indefinitely many such spaces? Or is it a singular 'quasi-holy' place, a particular geographical location where devotees of Wagner can gather to venerate the Master and faithfully re-enact his works according to the style and pattern he established? There is also this further question. In what way are the events on stage at Bayreuth related to ordinary life? The story of Christ's Crucifixion and Resurrection is not one that I can emulate, but that is of no consequence because it is the cosmic history of 'what the Lord has done for me'. The story of Tristan and Isolde is hardly one that I can be expected to emulate either, but it is a mythological narrative, not a cosmic history. The hero affirms the grandeur of his life by sacrificing it for the object of his love; but the grandeur of *my* life cannot be secured by the actions of a fictional hero.

Scruton finds deep mysteries at work on Wagner's stage, and remarks, correctly, that we must understand mysteries not by argument but by participation. 'It is to this act of participation that the Wagnerian music drama invites us, just as we are invited to the altar in the sacred ritual of a religious gathering' (Scruton 2004: 7). But what is the form of this participation? The Christian submits to personal baptism, joins in songs of praise and acts of worship, *consumes* the sacrament of the altar as a way of living 'in' Christ 'who lives and reigns for ever and ever in union with God the Father and the Holy Spirit, Amen'. All these actions find their celebratory summation in the festival of Easter. What actions of ordinary people can find their summation in opera? The question immediately points to a sharp contrast between the two cases, the difference in fact between a congregation and an audience. Whereas the members of a congregation are as much at prayer as those who lead them, the audience at an opera sits and watches. Most importantly, at the end it applauds the performers, and thus concurs in a separation of the two in a way that priest is never separated from people.

THE DANCE OF LIFE

It is just this transformation—from participants into audience—that Nietzsche deplored in the evolution of Greek tragedy. Having been a communal festival in which the whole city was united, it became a drama with actors and spectators. Once again, the historical accuracy of his account is not of any special consequence. It is the distinction this leads him to draw, between the Apollonian and the Dionysian, that is of interest. Contrary to any impression that the concept of *Gesamtkunstwerk* might give, the experience of the audience at one of Wagner's operas is essentially Apollonian—entrancement by an image, not possession by a spirit. In so far as one of these operas does communicate something of a 'religion of humanity', like Surrealist painting, it can do so only in the form of an 'epiphanic moment'. Perhaps such experience can instil 'a renewed sense of human life and purpose' (Scruton), and leave us feeling that the world is 'both brighter and less burdensome' (Gadamer), but any satisfactory re-enchantment of the world has to be more than episodic. Like a living religion properly so called, it must be able to pervade existence, able to be something that colours the way we live day by day, even if its doing so is relatively rare. This is what Schleiermacher means to emphasize with his insistence that 'religious feelings should accompany every human deed like a holy music'. The question is what 'music' might accompany our every deed when we have left the Wagnerian theatre.

There is a philosophy of life that we might call 'aestheticism'. Its best-known advocate, at least at some phases of his life, was Oscar Wilde. Wilde's commitment to flippancy makes it a view that is easily dismissed, but other more substantial thinkers have espoused elements of something similar. Edmund Burke, for example, in his defence of the aristocrats of pre-revolutionary France, contends that, though their indifference to the lot of the poor was from one point of view certainly reprehensible, their behaviour lost *most* of its vice by losing *all* its ugliness. The supposition behind this claim is that beauty can be redemptive of other faults. In short, style matters. At the same time, the extension of this idea beyond some limited cases (politeness, for example) leads to a concept of 'holy music' that is entirely superficial, something that, like paint or wallpaper, merely clothes the thing it decorates, and has no influence whatsoever on its nature. Such a conception would be wholly unsatisfactory applied to religion, because it would deny it any redemptive power. Conventional pieties are not true religion. By the same token, aestheticism cannot provide us with a satisfactory concept of post-religious re-enchantment. If all that Art has to offer the conduct of ordinary life is style, then it offers nothing that allows us to 'transcend' the limitations of the human condition in any interesting sense.

The aestheticism of style is no less Apollonian than the art of the epiphanic moment. Indeed, it is worse, because the style it recommends is apprehended by those who see it, not those who adopt it. I am not a witness to my own elegance. Perhaps, then, we should turn to the Dionysian. In *Nietzsche's Dancers*, Kimerer L. LaMothe draws attention to the striking number of places throughout his writings where Nietzsche refers to 'dance' and 'dancing'. On the strength of this LaMothe wants to forge a connection between the Nietzschean project of a revaluation of all values and the actual practice of dancing as exemplified in Isadora Duncan, Martha Graham, and others. Her efforts in this direction are not entirely convincing to my mind, but she unquestionably shows that the image of the dance is one that Nietzsche finds particularly congenial in the exposition and elaboration of his central idea.

What is unclear, very often, is whether he means to use it as a metaphor, an analogy, an instance of some general kind, or an important phenomenon in its own right. We can say this much, however. In its own right, dance is a phenomenon of considerable interest for present purposes, because it is a modest *Gesamtkunst-werk*. Combining and realizing the plastic, musical, dramatic, and performing arts, the dancer is to be contrasted with the spectator of visual, sonic, and literary art, as one engaged in action and not merely observation. As LaMothe says: 'The experience of dancing allows a person to sense and experience his own body differently. In the act of dancing, he is not only a body; he is a body making images of himself, kinetic images. He is a body *becoming* the kinetic images he *makes of himself*' (LaMothe 2006: 27, emphasis added).

While this picture is of a solitary dancer, dancing has a further important social dimension. It is an activity in which human beings hold and touch each other, and yet it is quite different from the physical engagement and interaction that are normally confined to the relationships of parent and child, husband and wife, lover and lover. But neither is it like the physical engagement of wrestlers. Dancers hold and touch in stylized 'steps', and thus uniquely enjoy a close collaborative physical contact with other human beings that is nonetheless without intimacy.

This last feature is one aspect of a deeper underlying character that dance has. It is a form of activity by which we are enabled to master some of the forces to which we are subject. This is the sense in which dance is a sort of 'overcoming'. In illustration of a similar point, Nietzsche elsewhere uses the example of the tightrope walker (in German a 'rope-dancer'). Suspended on a thin cord high above a precipice, the tightrope walker exploits the laws of physics to which human bodies are subject in order to accomplish something that those same laws would seem to make impossible. In a similar fashion, the ordinary dancer submits to the pulsating spirit of Dionysus, but in a way that transforms him from possessed to creator. As when water is driven through a water wheel, a force of nature is turned to an end that nature does not know.

Suppose we treat this as a metaphor for the way in which one might lead a life. What implications are we to draw? The first is this. Dance is pure activity. What we learn speculatively or practically may be put to use, but dance as such is not *about* anything, and it is not *for* anything. The dancer has no necessary beliefs, and accomplishes no purpose other than the dance itself. To this extent the metaphor of the 'dance of life' satisfies Schleiermacher's requirement that religion must be something sharply differentiated from the 'sphere and character of speculation as well as from that of praxis' (Schleiermacher 1799/1996: 23). Dance too, it seems, can show itself 'as the necessary and indispensable third next to those two, as their natural counterpart, not slighter in worth and splendour'. In other words, the dancer is unburdened of *both* theoretical commitments (whether theological or scientific) *and* utilitarian concerns. This is the profound freedom of dance. Schopenhauer could only conceive of freedom as release from the *principium individuationis*. 'True salvation, redemption from life and suffering', he tells us, 'cannot even be imagined without total denial of the will. Till then, everyone is nothing but this will itself, whose manifestation is an ephemeral existence, and always vain, constantly frustrated endeavour' (Schopenhauer 1819/1995: 250). In dance, as in (some forms of) religious worship, there is activity without will, and hence the release that Schopenhauer wants from the perpetually frustrated desire to be this or that, not through annihilation, but in the freedom simply to *be*. Thus, in the pure activity of dance, at one and the same time we realize *and* celebrate ourselves as human.

It remains to say, of course, just how this metaphor of the 'dance of life' is to be cashed out. What does all this mean for human conduct day to day? How are the necessary actions of ordinary life to be turned into 'a dance'? These are evidently pressing questions, and yet it is possible to get some further critical purchase on the metaphor without investigating them too deeply, because a more telling issue is this. Is everyone a dancer, or only those who are special masters of the art? Is the dance of life, like the tightrope walk, a rare accomplishment of a gifted few? Or can everyone and anyone be a dancer? Neither alternative seems attractive. The first would leave the world disenchanted for almost all of us. The second would make our self-salvation too easy to be of any consequence. This is a dilemma that is worth exploring further.

In *Fear and Trembling*, Kierkegaard, like Nietzsche, invokes the image of dance as a way of articulating contrasting modes of existence, in this case the life of 'infinite resignation' versus the life of 'faith'.

It is said that the dancer's hardest task is to leap straight into a definite position, so that not for a second does he have to catch at the position but stands there in it in the leap itself. Perhaps no dancer can do it—but that knight [of faith] does it. The mass of human beings live disheartened lives of earthly sorrow and joy, these are the sitters-out who will not join in the dance. The knights of infinity are dancers too and they have elevation. They make the upward movement and fall down again, and this too is no unhappy pastime, nor ungracious to behold. But when they come down they cannot assume the position straightaway, they waver an instant and the wavering shows they are nevertheless strangers in the world. This may be more or less evident, depending on their skill, but even the most skilled of the knights cannot hide the vacillation. But to be able to land in just that way, and in the same second to look as though one were up and walking, to transform the leap in life into a gait, to express the sublime in the pedestrian absolutely—that is something only the knight of faith can do—and it is the one and only marvel. (Kierkegaard 1843/1985: 70)

Kierkegaard here distinguishes between the dancers and the sitters-out, but also between two types of dancer. The difference is not altogether clear, though part of it seems to be this. The 'knights of infinity' struggle self-consciously to live life according to 'a philosophy', but their attempts to do so always falter in some little detail. Life itself throws up some obstacle, however small, so that they 'waver an instant and the wavering shows they are nevertheless strangers in the world'. The knights of faith are faultless dancers, which is to say, completely at home in the world, but the mark of their being so is that they can 'express the sublime in the pedestrian absolutely'. This raises the following question, however. If the mark of being at home in the world is 'the pedestrian absolutely', what is it that distinguishes the knight of faith from the sitter-out, who is thoroughly pedestrian by choosing not to dance at all? The knight of faith's move from leap to gait is so smooth, it is as though he never leapt at all. That seems to be what commends it. But how, then, are we to discriminate between the knight of faith and the sitter-out? Changing the metaphor back to Schleiermacher's, we might ask: how can the life of the knight of faith be accompanied by 'a holy music', if the music sounds no different from the tunes of everyday?

There is a risk here that the philosophical question in which we are interested becomes too deeply embroiled in metaphor. So let us try to state the issue in a more straightforward way. At one level, it is not hard to tell the religious person from the non-religious person. The first goes in for practices that the second does not. Of course, it is correct to say that such practices can be engaged merely out of custom or convention, which is to say without the spirit of faith, and faithless religion is the phenomenon with which Kierkegaard is chiefly concerned (some might say 'obsessed'). It is also Nietzsche's aim to point to the conventional behaviour of a 'dead' religion, though from a somewhat different perspective. Faithless religion is common enough, and equally empty whether true faith remains a possibility or not. Yet at some point the 'faithful' (be they serious or deluded) act in ways that humanists do not—they engage in worship, prayer, sacrifice, and so on. The point, and effect, of these actions is to relate those who perform them to the fact of their existence in distinctive ways. Thus, thanking God is a response to thinking of life as a gift, and thinking of it as a gift is the ground for thanking God. Similarly, the worshipper stands in awe before the sacred—that is, the boundaries within which our existence is confined, and beyond which is dark mystery. The act of worship is an acknowledgement of the sacred, and the sacred thus orients the act of worship. If we follow Kierkegaard and use the metaphor of 'the dance' to characterize the life of religious faith, rather than following Nietzsche in using it to capture a post-religious alternative, we can say that the religious 'dance' life differently, and we can point to these practices as their distinctive dance steps. But what of the humanist? What practices constitute the distinctive steps in an alternative dance?

THE TRANSFIGURATION OF THE COMMONPLACE

The idea we have been exploring throughout this book is that we should look to the arts (having won their autonomy from religion) to provide the answer to this question. The humanistic 'dance of life' can turn to painting, music, storytelling, and the art of building as modes in which the human spirit realizes its own inspiring creativity, and can thereby liberate itself from the lingering desire for supernatural agencies. Previous chapters raised significant doubts about the extent to which this is a plausible ambition for arts, whose autonomy has been achieved through ever greater degrees of aesthetic self-consciousness. One evident effect of this self-consciousness, perhaps an essential aspect of it, is a large measure of cultural isolation. Modern 'high' art is largely cut off from common life in a way that sport, say, is not. This cultural isolation is reflected in the frequency with which the question 'but is it art?' is raised with respect to contemporary art exhibits. It signals a gulf between the aesthetic preferences of the art world and those of the general public. This gulf was illustrated most dramatically in the Komar and Melamid experiment of *America's Most Wanted* (1994). This was a painting deliberately constructed on the basis of social-survey research into aesthetic preferences, and it differed just about as much as could be from the self-generated works of the contemporary art world—a pastoral lakeside scene with deer and figures in eighteenth-century costume and blue mountains beyond.

The question 'but is it art?', like the judgement 'a child could have done that', naturally arises where, it seems, anything we might call artistry is conspicuously lacking. Yet, importantly, a feature of the modern art world is its positive classification of readymades (and multiples) as 'works of art'. Starting in 1917 with Duchamp's urinal entitled *Fountain*, a sequence of famous 'works' has followed, of which Warhol's *Brillo Box* is probably the most famous. It was encountering *Brillo Box* that started the philosopher Arthur Danto on a long process of philosophical reflection, beginning with *The Transfiguration of the Commonplace* (1981) and culminating in *After the End of Art*, first given as the Mellon Lectures in Fine Art for 1995. This second volume is subtitled 'Contemporary Art and the Pale of History', and in it Danto endorses a sort of Hegelianism about art—namely, the view that the result of art's historical development is its end or completion. However, whereas Hegel concludes from this that Spirit can no longer satisfactorily realize itself in Art and must thus pass on to other modes or media (namely, Religion and then Philosophy), for Danto the completion of art is not its exhaustion. On the contrary, in his view all art is now liberated from its historical, and institutional, confinement.

There are no a priori constraints on what a work of visual art can look like, so that anything visible can be a visual work. That is part of what it really means to live at the end of art history. This means in particular that it is altogether possible for artists to appropriate the forms of past art, and use to their own expressive ends the cave painting, the altarpiece, the baroque portrait, the cubist landscape, Chinese landscape in the Sung style, or whatever . . . . It is not possible to relate to these works as those did in whose form of life those works played the role they played: we are not cavemen, nor are we devout mediaevals, baroque princelings, Parisian bohemians on the frontiers of a new style, or Chinese literati. Of course, no period can relate to the art of earlier life-forms in the way those who lived those life-forms did. But neither could they, as we can, make those forms ours. There is a difference to be drawn between the forms and the way we relate to them. The sense in which everything is possible is that in which all forms are ours. (Danto 1997: 198)

As the opening sentence of this passage makes plain, 'everything is possible', not just in the appropriation of all and any art forms from the past, but in the 'appropriation' of any object at all as a 'work of art'. Nor is this appropriation confined to the acknowledged experts of the art world or the keepers of famous art museums. Reflecting on *We Got It!*, a chocolate candy bar produced at the 1993 Chicago *Culture in Action* exhibition by the Bakery, Confectionery, and Tobacco Workers' International Union of America, Local No. 552, and described in the text as 'The Candy of their Dreams', Danto is quite willing to acknowledge it as a work of art. 'A candy bar that is a work of art need not be some especially good candy bar. It just has to be a candy bar produced with the intention that it be art' (ibid. 185). This remarkable effect is possible because of the 'conceptual revolutions in art' that marked the twentieth century. It is these that have made possible, alongside museum art, community-based 'art of their own' like *We Got It!* Danto's reflections lead him to a speculation about what might ultimately happen 'after the end of art'.

It is possible to suppose that the kind of art the museum defines has had its day and that we have lived into a revolution in the concept of art as remarkable as the revolution with which that concept emerged, say around 1400, and which made the museum an institution exactly suited to art of that kind. I myself argue here, and in a number of places, that the end of art has come, meaning that the narrative generated by that concept has come to its internally projected end. When art changes, the museum may fall away as the fundamental aesthetic institution, and extramuseal exhibitions of the sort *Culture in Action* exemplifies, in which art and life are far more closely intertwined than the conventions of the museum allows, may become the norm. (ibid. 187)

It is the emergence of this 'art of their own' that dramatically extends the 'transfiguration of the commonplace' that *Brillo Box* and the like constituted in their day. Now, as it seems to me, if art is to re-enchant the world, a 'transfiguration of the commonplace' is exactly what is required. The crucial question, though, is how we are to tell that such a transfiguration has been accomplished, and not just pretended or imagined. The simple intention that a candy bar be art seems much too weak because it presupposes that we know, independently of the candy bar, the community, or the museum, what it is that is intended. What makes this a crucial issue is the fact that the evidence for the enriching 'conceptual revolution' in art that Danto appeals to is the very same evidence that other critics use to establish the bankruptcy of art. In a lecture delivered at the Tate Gallery in London in the same year that Danto delivered his Mellon Lectures (though ranging more widely than the visual arts), Roger Scruton sees in the sort of development Danto applauds 'a sudden and catastrophic impoverishment of the artistic intention, and a launching of abstract art towards the scribbles of Twombly, and the mournful bombast of Rothko'. 'Equally damaging', he thinks, 'has been the tendency of art—and abstract art in particular—to invade the surrounding space, to colonize every available inch of floor, wall or ceiling, in order to drive out from our perceptions all that is not art, all that is merely homely, decorative, and unassuming' (Scruton 1996: 346). The upshot is not a transfiguration of the commonplace by artistic intention, but kitsch.

Kitsch art is art produced by someone who has no idea what art is—of its expressive and spiritual potential—but who seeks by artistic means to falsify reality and to confirm a habit of emotional laziness. The world of kitsch is a world of winsome make-believe, of sugary promises, of instant reward; and kitsch itself is pseudo-art—art which pretends to a status which it cannot acquire. Its repulsive quality lies in the invitation to join in its self-deception, to lower ourselves, as though in ingratiating company to a complicity of pretence. (ibid.)

There can be little doubt that by these criteria *We Got It!* is kitsch—pseudo-art that pretends to a status that it cannot acquire (perhaps more accurately, pseudo-art on whose behalf this claim is made by theorists). It would be a mistake to suggest, however, that Scruton wishes to confine art to the gallery. On the contrary:

The artistic enterprise must . . . build bridges to the world of popular feeling—not by endorsing what is lowest in popular culture, but enobling what is genuine. The task before us is the opposite of that which appealed to Warhol and Koons: we are not here to place inverted commas round trash, and so make a joke of nothingness. We must descend into the world of cliché and rescue it for human life. (ibid. 349)

My purpose here is not to take sides with Danto or Scruton on this issue, but to point up the fact that the phenomena of modern art can plausibly be made to sustain diametrically opposed positions. According to Scruton, 'no more than our predecessors, can we accept the view of our lives as transitory, futile and empty of meaning' (ibid.), and he looks to art (at least in part) as one of the ways in which such futility is to be circumvented. This is a thought with which Danto would concur. But, whereas Danto sees 'art of their own' as the way in which the redemptive power of the high art of the past is extended to the pop art of the present, Scruton interprets the very same world as one in which, precisely because 'art and pop exist on the same level . . . the fact that we are surrounded by rubbish becomes less easy to perceive' (ibid. 347). In what is (presumably) a deliberate amendment to Danto, Scruton looks to art for 'the redemption of the commonplace' (ibid.), and not merely its transfiguration. So we are back with our dilemma. Is the re-enchantment of the world through art a rare accomplishment of a gifted few? Or is it, as Joseph Beuys contended, 'that anything could be a work of art [and] everyone... an artist' (quoted in Danto 1997: 184)? If, prompted by Nietzsche, it is active artistic engagement, and not merely passive observation, that we have in view, the first leaves the world disenchanted for almost all of us, while the second makes our self-salvation too easy to be of any consequence.

This result arises from a modern ambition, evidenced in all the arts, to 'break down' the barrier between 'art' and 'life'. Two of the figures Scruton castigates—Twombly and Rothko—are identified with the movement known as 'abstract expressionism' that made this one of its key ideas. A counterpart is to be found in music, notably the music of John Cage (an important influence on Twombly). Cage's most famous 'work' is *4′3″*, in which the pianist sits at a piano for four minutes and thirty-three seconds but does not play, simply rising at the end to take applause. Any 'gulf' between music and the world of everyday sound is certainly broken down here, and this is part of Cage's point—that we should give to the chance combination of sounds around us the kind of attention we give to deliberately composed sound. The problem is that in *4′3″* the difference has not been overcome; it has simply been eliminated. If 'music' of this kind is the secular equivalent of the 'holy music' with which Schleiermacher thinks religion makes life meaningful, it is indistinguishable from silence, which is to say no music at all.

This is no unhappy accident, but a natural outcome of art's ambition to re-enchant the world. Religion accompanies human life in rites of passage and in festival seamlessly. Moreover, it can deploy the arts to this end with great ease—Christmas carols, funeral anthems, church weddings, icons and vestments. If art alone is to emulate religion in this respect, it does seem that the boundary between high art and ordinary life has to be broken down in some way. Once the barriers are down, however, the result can as easily be the reduction of art as the elevation of life, and the 'transfiguration of the commonplace' an illusion generated by wishful thinking and sustained by the conventional wisdom of the art world. Perhaps this 'disenchantment of art' is not inevitable, but it is an evident danger that has not yet been avoided.

Conclusion

Let us consider a painting once described by the Danish wit Søren Kierkegaard. It was a painting of the Israelites crossing the Red Sea. Looking at it, one would have seen something very different from what a painting with that subject would have led one to expect, were one to imagine, for example, what an artist like Poussin or Altdorfer would have painted: troops of people, in various postures of panic, bearing the burdens of their dislocated lives, and in the distance the horsed might of the Egyptian forces bearing down. Here, instead, was a square of red paint, the artist explaining that 'The Israelites had already crossed over, and the Egyptians were drowned'. Kierkegaard comments that the result of his life is like that painting. All the spiritual turmoil, the father cursing God on the heath, the rupture with Regina Olsen, the inner search for Christian meaning, the sustained polemics of an agonized soul, meld in the end, as in the echoes of the Marabar Caves, into 'a mood, a single color'. (Danto 1981: 1)

This episode, recounted by Danto at the opening of *The Transfiguration of the Commonplace*, may reflect Kierkegaard's familiarity with Schopenhauer. In *The World as Will and Idea*, Schopenhauer advances the highly novel view that music is the most profound of all the arts, since it is 'a copy of the will itself' (Schopenhauer 1819/1995: 164). 'Melody', he tells us, is 'the disclosure of all the deepest secrets of human willing and feeling' (ibid. 167). But it is crucial for us to understand that 'the nature of melody is a constant digression and deviation from the key-note in a thousand ways . . . yet there always follows a return at last to the key-note' (ibid. 167). What we should conclude from this is that, just as it is only melody and not a sustained key-note that is worth listening to, any respite from human striving can result only in '*ennui*', 'the empty longing for a new desire' (ibid.). That is why Schopenhauer himself endorses 'the surrender and denial of that will [as] the only possible deliverance from the world and its miseries' (ibid. 229).

Schopenhauer's asceticism relies on his pessimism, and it cannot easily be made to cohere with his philosophy of the will. But we can abandon both, and still find in his writing an independent view of death and its survival, one that makes no appeal to the need for a 'surrender and denial' of the will that drives us. Rather, like Schleiermacher, he sees the fear of death and hope for personal immortality as resting on a profound misunderstanding, the mistake of taking the phenomenal to be the reality of which it is merely a manifestation. The only immortality it makes any sense to seek, is an identification with 'the one will to life' that is manifested by the world 'in all the plurality of its parts and forms' (Schopenhauer 1819/1995: 216). It we take this view, and without the additional thought that 'all life is suffering', it is open to us to *rejoice* in the mere fact of the will to life operative within us, to exercise it to the full for as long as it lasts, and to seek ways in which to celebrate our doing so. This is, I think, the attitude that Nietzsche ultimately recommends, and he is unafraid to add that this joyful affirmation of the will should ignore all the normal constraints that morality would have us place upon it.

And yet even Nietzsche seems, in the end, to search for something more, some further mark of significance, which he finds in the test of 'eternal recurrence'. This is a test of enduring value. It is invoked because the thought that proves so difficult for human beings to accept is that the achievements that we find most significant, and in which we take most pride, should, at the end, amount to nothing much. That is the point of Kierkegaard's reflection on the picture of the Red Sea. Can it be that the ultimate outcome of such a dramatic story, a Chosen People's deliverance from slavery by divine command, can be summarized in a monochrome patch of red? Schopenhauer makes a closely related point when he remarks elsewhere that novels never recount the period in which the protagonists 'lived happily ever after' (Schopenhauer 1819/1995: 203). To do so, like playing just the key-note with which a melody ends, would be to guarantee the onset of *ennui*. Confined to the perspective of the story, 'the happy ending' is really just 'the end', and there is no 'ever after'.

All this is, we might say, 'so far as we can see'. Every religion of any sophistication either implicitly assumes or expressly teaches that beyond our horizons there are other realms. These are the realms of the sacred, and, though they must ultimately remain mysteries, this is not the same as saying we must remain in ignorance of them. The accumulated practices of religion are ways in which we are enabled to encounter the sacred, in Schleiermacher's language to 'intuit the infinite', and thus to make the sacred the frame within which our lives are set, and in the context of which they then take their meaning. From the religious point of view, we are creatures under Providence, or Judgement, or some such concept. In the absence of the sacred, there is no frame of reference other than that which human beings prove capable of providing for themselves. But this is tantamount to saying, more simply, that there is no frame within which human life *has* to be lived. The only thing we are compelled to acknowledge is the important, but meaningless, limit set by the contingencies of the natural world. Each human life, in this case, just *is* a passage of time from the cradle to the grave.

A collect in the *Book of Common Prayer* asks God to let us 'pass our time in rest and quietness'. This may reflect an anxiety about civil unrest contemporaneous to its composition, as well as a culture less driven by the demands of accomplishment and achievement than ours. But, if we take this at face value, we can of course aspire to more than this. There can be more to life than 'amusing ourselves to death', and not just the work required for earning the means to do so. Generally speaking, the arts provide something more. In addition to the merely entertaining, painting, music, literature, and the built environment stock the world with beauty, interest, the clever, and the captivating. Yet, all this falls squarely within Schopenhauer's realm of 'the will', and, if the arguments of this book are sound, nothing in the arts provides the means by which we might transcend it. Painting alone will never let us see the sacred; fiction as such provides no cosmic pattern of life; music alone has developed in a direction that eliminates the Dionysian altogether. And, while we can build ourselves a different type of sacred space, we lack the right kind of festival with which to fill it. In short, the abandonment of religion, it seems, must mean the permanent disenchantment of the world, and any ambition on the part of art to remedy this is doomed to failure.

In the light of this conclusion, ought anyone to be depressed or distressed? Perhaps the 'cultured despisers' should. But one further thought is this. Almost all the philosophers whose writings have been drawn upon in the preceding discussion are thinking within the nineteenth century's philosophy of history. This conceives of the past as a progressive development, and places Europe at its cutting edge. Consequently, it implies, what Europe experiences today, the rest of the world will experience tomorrow, or shortly after. But the phenomenon of globalization, and with it an awareness of the power and presence of religion in the modern world, ought to alert us to the possibility that the idea of secularization, and the related debate about the consequences of secularism, may be a relatively local, and even minor, affair, confined to two centuries of European history. If so, what autonomous Art has set itself (and been called upon) to remedy is a partial, and probably temporary, condition, about which there is no cause to be excessively exercised.

Religion as a sphere of meaning can articulate such a thought without difficulty. The human spirit may for a time forget, but instinctively knows that, as Augustine puts it, 'our hearts are restless till they rest in Thee'.

References

This References section contains all the works discussed or referred to in the text. Where two dates of publication appear in parentheses after the author's name, the first refers to the original date of publication and the second to the date of the translation/edition that has been used and/or quoted.

Aikman, David (2004). *Jesus in Beijing: How Christianity is Transforming China and Changing the Global Balance of Power.* Washington: Regnery Publishing.

Arnold, Matthew (1880/1964). *Essays in Criticism: First and Second Series.* Everyman's Library; London: J. M. Dent.

Austin, J. L. (1961). 'Performative Utterances', in *Philosophical Papers.* Oxford: Oxford University Press.

Barzun, Jacques (1974). *The Use and Abuse of Art.* Princeton: Princeton University Press.

Berger, Karol (2002). *A Theory of Art.* Oxford and New York: Oxford University Press.

Bradley, Fiona (1997). *Surrealism.* London: Tate Gallery Publishing.

Brown, Callum G. (2003). *The Death of Christian Britain: Understanding Secularization.* London and New York: Routledge.

Budd, Malcolm (1985). *Music and the Emotions: The Philosophical Theories.* London: Routledge & Kegan Paul.

Caird, Edward (1907). *The Evolution of Religion.* 2 vols.; Glasgow: James Maclehose and Sons, publishers to the University.

Chadwick, Owen (1975). *The Secularization of the European Mind in the Nineteenth Century.* Cambridge: Cambridge University Press.

Collingwood, R. G. (1938/1974). *The Principles of Art.* Oxford: Clarendon Press.

Cupitt, Don (1984). *The Sea of Faith.* London: BBC Books.

Danto, Arthur C. (1981). *The Transfiguration of the Commonplace.* Cambridge, Mass.: Harvard University Press.

―― (1997). *After the End of Art: Contemporary Art and the Pale of History.* Princeton: Princeton University Press.

188   *References*

Darwin, Charles (1872). *Origin of Species.* 6th edn.; London: John Murray.

Frazer, Sir James George (1922/1957). *The Golden Bough: A Study in Magic and Religion.* Abridged paperback edn.; London and Basingstoke: Macmillan.

Gadamer, Hans-Georg (1967/1986). *The Relevance of the Beautiful and Other Essays,* ed. Robert Bernasconi. Cambridge: Cambridge University Press.

Graham, Gordon (2001). *Evil and Christian Ethics.* Cambridge: Cambridge University Press.

——(2005). *Philosophy of the Arts: An Introduction to Aesthetics.* 3rd edn.; London and New York: Routledge.

——(2007). 'Music and Electro-Sonic Art', in Kathleen Stock (ed.), *Meaning, Experience and Work: Philosophers on Music.* Oxford: Oxford University Press.

Greene, Graham (1992). *Stamboul Train: An Entertainment.* Penguin Twentieth-Century Classics; London, Penguin.

Hanslick, Eduard (1926/1986). *On the Musically Beautiful,* trans. Geoffrey Payzant. Indianapolis: Hackett Publishing Company.

Harries, Karsten (1997). *The Ethical Function of Architecture.* Cambridge, Mass.: MIT Press.

Hegel, G. W. F. (1975). *Hegel's Aesthetics: Lectures on Fine Art,* trans. T. M. Knox. 2 vols.; Oxford: Clarendon Press.

——(1980). *Lectures on the Philosophy of World History: Introduction,* trans. H. B. Nisbet. Cambridge: Cambridge University Press.

Hess, Barbara, and Grosenick, Uta (2005). *Abstract Expressionism.* Cologne: Taschen.

Hume, David (1779/1947). *Dialogues concerning Natural Religion,* ed. Norman Kemp Smith. 2nd edn. London and Edinburgh: Thomas Nelson and Sons.

John of Damascus (726/2003). *Three Treatises on the Divine Images,* trans. and introd. Andrew Louth. Crestwood, NY: St Vladimir's Seminary Press.

Joyce, James (2000). *Ulysses,* intro. Declan Kiberd. Penguin Modern Classics; London: Penguin.

——(2003a). *Portrait of the Artist as a Young Man,* intro. Seumas Deane. Penguin Modern Classics; London: Penguin.

——(2003b). *Dubliners,* intro. Jeri Johnson. World Classics; Oxford: Oxford University Press.

Kandinsky, Wassily (1947/1963). *Concerning the Spiritual in Art*. New York: Dover.

Kant, Immanuel (1790/3, 2001). *Critique of the Power of Judgment*, trans. Paul Guyer. Cambridge: Cambridge University Press.

Kekes, John (2002). *The Art of Life*. Ithaca, NY: Cornell University Press.

—— (2005). *The Roots of Evil*. Ithaca, NY: Cornell University Press.

Kennedy, Michael (1996) (ed.), *The Concise Oxford Dictionary of Music*. Oxford Reference On-line; Oxford: Oxford University Press.

Kepel, Gilles (1991/1994). *The Revenge of God: The Resurgence of Islam, Christianity and Judaism in the Modern World*, University Park, Pa.: Pennsylvania State University Press.

Kieran, Matthew (2006) (ed.). *Contemporary Debates in Aesthetics and the Philosophy of Art*. Oxford: Blackwell.

Kierkegaard, Søren (1843/1985). *Fear and Trembling*, ed. and trans. Alastair Hannay. Harmondsworth: Penguin.

—— (1992). *Concluding Unscientific Postscript to Philosophical Fragments*, ed. and trans. Howard V. Hong and Edna H. Hong. 2 vols.; Princeton: Princeton University Press.

Kivy, Peter (1991). *Music Alone: Philosophical Reflections on Purely Musical Experience*. Ithaca, NY: Cornell University Press.

—— (1993). *The Fine Art of Repetition: Essays in the Philosophy of Music*. Cambridge: Cambridge University Press.

Klingsöhr-Leroy, Cathrin (2004). *Surrealism*. Cologne: Taschen.

Kolakowski, Leszek (1990). *Modernity on Endless Trial*. Chicago: University of Chicago Press.

Kuspit, Donald (2004), *The End of Art*. Cambridge: Cambridge University Press.

LaMothe, Kimerer L. (2006). *Nietzsche's Dancers: Isadora Duncan, Martha Graham, and the Revaluation of Christian Values*. New York: Palgrave Macmillan.

Leaver, Robin (2004). 'Bach and Religion', in *Cambridge Companion to Bach*, ed. John Butt. Cambridge: Cambridge University Press.

Levinson, Jerrold (2003) (ed.). *The Oxford Handbook of Aesthetics*. Oxford: Oxford University Press.

MacIntyre, Alasdair (1981). *After Virtue: A Study in Moral Theory*. London: Gerald Duckworth.

Mattick, Paul (1944/2003). *Art in its Time: Theories and Practices of Modern Aesthetics*. London: Routledge.

Murdoch, Iris (1970). *The Sovereignty of Good*. London: Routledge and Kegan Paul.

Nes, Solrunn (2004). *The Mystical Language of Icons*. Grand Rapids, Mich.: William B. Eerdmans.

Nietzsche, Friedrich (1886/1993). *The Birth of Tragedy*, trans. Shaun Whiteside, ed. Michael Tanner. London: Penguin Books.

—— (1887/2001). *The Gay Science*, ed. Bernard Williams, trans. Josefine Nauckhoff. 2nd edn.; Cambridge: Cambridge University Press.

—— (1878/2004), *Human, All Too Human*, trans. Marion Faber and Stephen Lehmann. London: Penguin Books.

Oakeshott, Michael (1933), *Experience and its Modes*. Cambridge: Cambridge University Press.

Pevsner, Nikolaus (1963). *An Outline of European Architecture*. 7th edn.; New York: Scribner.

Phillips, D. Z. (1976). *Religion without Explanation*. Oxford: Basil Blackwell.

Prichard, Robert (1991). *A History of the Episcopal Church*. Harrisburg, Pa.: Morehouse Publishing.

Rabinovitch, Celia (2004). *Surrealism and the Sacred: Power, Eros, and the Occult in Modern Art*. Boulder, Colo.: Westview Press.

Ritchie, D.G. (1893/1998). *Darwin and Hegel: With Other Philosophical Studies*, ed. and intro. Peter P. Nicholson. Bristol: Thoemmes Press.

Ricœur, Paul (1991). 'Life in Quest of Narrative', in *On Paul Ricœur: Narrative and Interpretation*, ed. David Wood. London: Routledge.

Rookmaaker, H. R. (1970/1994). *Modern Art and the Death of a Culture*. Wheaton, Ill.: Crossway Books.

Rogers, Ben (2004) (ed.). *Is Nothing Sacred?* London and New York: Routledge.

Schleiermacher, Friedrich (1799/1996). *On Religion: Speeches to its Cultured Despisers*, ed. Richard Crouter. Cambridge: Cambridge University Press.

Schopenhauer, Arthur (1819/1995). *The World as Will and Idea*, ed. David Berman, trans. Jill Berman. London: Everyman.

Scruton, Roger (1996). 'The Aesthetic Endeavour Today', *Philosophy*, 71: 331–50.

—— (2004). *Death-Devoted Heart: Sex and the Sacred in Wagner's* Tristan and Isolde. Oxford: Oxford University Press.

—— (2006). *Gentle Regrets*. London. Continuum.

Shiner, Larry (2001). *The Invention of Art: A Cultural History*. Chicago: University of Chicago Press.

Styan, J. L. (1981). *Modern Drama in Theory and Practice 2: Symbolism, Surrealism and the Absurd*. Cambridge: Cambridge University Press.

Tanner, Michael (1976–7). 'Sentimentality', *Proceedings of the Aristotelian Society*, NS 77: 127–47.

Thomas, Keith (1971/1978). *Religion and the Decline of Magic*. Harmondsworth: Penguin Books.

Tolstoy, Leo (1906). *Twenty Three Tales*, trans. Aylmer Maude. World's Classics; Oxford: Oxford University Press.

Weber, Max (1948/2004). *From Max Weber: Essays in Sociology*, ed. and intro. H. H. Gerth and C. Wright Mills. London: Routledge.

Wolterstorff, Nicholas (1980/1996). *Art in Action: Towards a Christian Aesthetic*. Grand Rapids, Mich.: William B. Eerdmans.

——— (1985). 'Art, Religion, and the Elite: Reflections on a Passage from André Malraux', in Diane Apostolos-Cappadona (ed.), *Art, Creativity, and the Sacred*. New York: Crossroads.

Index